FREE-FLOATING SUBDIVISIONS:

AN ALPHABETICAL INDEX

20TH EDITION

PREPARED BY

THE CATALOGING POLICY AND SUPPORT OFFICE

LIBRARY OF CONGRESS

CATALOGING DISTRIBUTION SERVICE

WASHINGTON, D.C. 2008

ISSN   1052-1445

PREFACE

The free-floating subdivisions used in Library of Congress subject headings appear in thirty-five separate lists in the *Subject Cataloging Manual: Subject Headings*. This index, compiled by the Cataloging Policy and Support Office, is a consolidated alphabetical listing of all free-floating subdivisions in the manual as well as newly-approved free-floating subdivisions not yet published in the manual. The first edition of the index was published in 1989. Subsequent editions have been published annually. This twentieth edition includes subdivisions approved through December 2007.

This list should be used as an index to the manual by those who wish to assign and retrieve free-floating subdivisions.

Barbara B. Tillett
Chief, Cataloging Policy and Support Office

January 2008

INTRODUCTION

This list consists of all free-floating subdivisions that appear in H 1095 - H 1200 in the current edition of the *Subject Cataloging Manual: Subject Headings*, and serves as an index to the free-floating subdivisions in that publication. This twentieth edition of the list is up to date through December 2007.

For each subdivision, a listing is provided of the free-floating lists in the manual where it appears, identified by category. Since the subdivisions that appear in H 1095 have no single, identifiable category, the user is directed, by the notation "see *SCM:SH*," to consult H 1095 in the *Subject Cataloging Manual* to determine appropriate usage. For subdivisions that have specific instruction sheets in the manual describing their usage, citations to these are provided in the column labeled "USAGE GUIDELINES IN SCM:SH."

The list includes a column providing the MARC 21 subfield codes that apply to each subdivision. The Library of Congress began applying subfield code **v** to form subdivisions in 1999. It should be noted that most subdivisions identified as form subdivisions and coded **v** in this publication may also be assigned as topical subdivisions to works that are about those bibliographical forms. In such cases, the subdivisions are coded in the bibliographic record as **x** rather than **v**. The coding provided here represents Library of Congress cataloging practice. Some subdivisions that may appear to be form subdivisions (such as –**Manuscripts**, –**Personnel records**, or –**Poetic works**) are coded **x** because the Library of Congress assigns them only to works that are *about* the form rather than to actual individual instances of the form. Other subdivisions that may appear to be topical (such as –**Congresses**, –**Identification**, or –**Pedigrees**) are coded **v** because the Library of Congress uses these subdivisions primarily to designate bibliographical forms (such as conference proceedings, identification guides, or pedigree books). The Library has made the decision to consistently treat certain problematic subdivisions such as –**History**, –**History and criticism**, and –**Law and legislation** as topical and always to code them **x**. A full explanation of the distinctions between topical, geographic, chronological, and form subdivisions is provided in the *Subject Cataloging Manual: Subject Headings*, 5th edition, H 1075, *Subdivisions*.

This list should be used with caution and only in conjunction with the *Subject Cataloging Manual*. After locating a subdivision in the list, it is usually necessary, particularly for those subdivisions listed in H 1095, to consult the manual to determine restrictions on its usage in specific situations. These are found in footnotes or scope notes on the free-floating lists in the manual or in an instruction sheet that provides usage guidelines. Restrictions of this type are not indicated in this list.

KEY TO TERMS USED UNDER "CATEGORY"

Term Used	Category Represented	SCM:SH #
Animals	Animals	H 1147
Art	Art	H 1148
Bodies water	Bodies of Water	H 1145.5
Chemicals	Chemicals	H 1149
Chinese art	Chinese Art	H 1148
Christian denom	Christian Denominations	H 1187
Classes pers	Classes of Persons	H 1100
Colonies	Colonies	H 1149.5
Corp bodies	Corporate Bodies	H 1105
Diseases	Diseases	H 1150
Drama	Drama	H 1156
Ethnic groups	Ethnic Groups	H 1103
Families	Individual Family Names	H 1120
Groups lit auth	Groups of Literary Authors	H 1155.2
Indiv pers	Names of Persons	H 1110
Indiv schools	Individual Educational Institutions	H 1151
Industries	Industries	H 1153
Japanese art	Japanese Art	H 1148
Korean art	Korean Art	H 1148
Land vehicles	Land Vehicles	H 1195
Languages	Languages	H 1154
Legal topics	Legal Topics	H 1154.5
Legis bodies	Legislative Bodies	H 1155
Lit works/Auth	Literary Works Entered Under Author	H 1155.6
Lit works/Title	Literary Works Entered Under Title	H 1155.8
Literatures	Literatures	H 1156
Materials	Materials	H 1158
Military srvces	Military Services	H 1159
Musical comps	Musical Compositions	H 1160
Musical instrum	Musical Instruments	H 1161
Organs of body	Organs and Regions of the Body	H 1164
Places	Names of Places	H 1140
Plants & crops	Plants and Crops	H 1180
Relig orders	Religious and Monastic Orders	H 1186
Religions	Religions	H 1185
Sacred works	Sacred Works	H 1188
see *SCM:SH*	No category; consult *Subject Cataloging Manual*	H 1095
Types schools	Types of Educational Institutions	H 1151.5
Wars	Wars	H 1200

SUBDIVISION	SUBFIELD CODE(S)	FREE-FLOATING LIST IN SCM:SH	CATEGORY	USAGE GUIDELINES IN SCM:SH
–2-harpsichord scores	v	H 1160	Musical comps	
–2-organ scores	v	H 1160	Musical comps	
–2-piano scores	v	H 1160	Musical comps	
–3-piano scores	v	H 1160	Musical comps	
–500-1400	y	H 1160	Musical comps	
–10th century	y	H 1148	Art	
–11th century	y	H 1148	Art	
–12th century	y	H 1148	Art	
–13th century	y	H 1148	Art	
–14th century	y	H 1148	Art	
–15th century	y	H 1148	Art	
		H 1160	Musical comps	
–16th century	y	H 1148	Art	
		H 1160	Musical comps	
–17th century	y	H 1148	Art	
		H 1156	Drama	
		H 1160	Musical comps	
–18th century	y	H 1148	Art	
		H 1154	Languages	
		H 1155.2	Groups lit auth	
		H 1156	Literatures	
		H 1156	Drama	
		H 1160	Musical comps	
–19th century	y	H 1148	Art	
		H 1148	Japanese art	
		H 1154	Languages	
		H 1155.2	Groups lit auth	
		H 1156	Literatures	
		H 1156	Drama	
		H 1160	Musical comps	
–1868-	y	H 1148	Japanese art	

SUBDIVISION	SUBFIELD CODE(S)	FREE-FLOATING LIST IN SCM:SH	CATEGORY	USAGE GUIDELINES IN SCM:SH	
–20th century	y	H 1148	Art		
		H 1148	Chinese art		
		H 1148	Japanese art		
		H 1148	Korean art		
		H 1154	Languages		
		H 1155.2	Groups lit auth		
		H 1156	Literatures		
		H 1156	Drama		
		H 1160	Musical comps		
–21st century	y	H 1148	Art		
		H 1148	Chinese art		
		H 1148	Japanese art		
		H 1148	Korean art		
		H 1154	Languages		
		H 1155.2	Groups lit auth		
		H 1156	Literatures		
		H 1156	Drama		
		H 1160	Musical comps		
–Abbreviations	x	H 1095	see *SCM:SH*		
–Abbreviations–Dictionaries	x–v	H 1095	see *SCM:SH*		
–Abbreviations of titles	v	H 1095	see *SCM:SH*		
–Abdication, [date]	x	H 1110	Indiv pers		
–Ability testing *(May Subd Geog)*	x	H 1095	see *SCM:SH*		
–Abnormalities *(May Subd Geog)*	x	H 1147	Animals		
		H 1164	Organs of body		
		H 1180	Plants & crops		
–Abridgments	v	H 1188	Sacred works		
–Abscess *(May Subd Geog)*	x	H 1164	Organs of body		
–Absolute constructions	x	H 1154	Languages		
–Absorption and adsorption *(May Subd Geog)*	x	H 1149	Chemicals		
–Abstracting and indexing *(May Subd Geog)*	x	H 1095	see *SCM:SH*	H 1205	H 1670
		H 1100	Classes pers	H 1205	H 1670
		H 1103	Ethnic groups	H 1205	H 1670
		H 1140	Places	H 1205	H 1670
		H 1188	Sacred works	H 1205	H 1670

SUBDIVISION	SUBFIELD CODE(S)	FREE-FLOATING LIST IN SCM:SH	CATEGORY	USAGE GUIDELINES IN SCM:SH
–Abstracts	v	H 1095	see *SCM:SH*	H 1205
		H 1100	Classes pers	H 1205
		H 1103	Ethnic groups	H 1205
		H 1105	Corp bodies	H 1205
		H 1110	Indiv pers	H 1205
		H 1140	Places	H 1205
–Abuse of *(May Subd Geog)*	x	H 1100	Classes pers	
–Accents and accentuation	x	H 1154	Languages	
		H 1188	Sacred works	
–Access control *(May Subd Geog)*	x	H 1095	see *SCM:SH*	
–Accidents *(May Subd Geog)*	x	H 1095	see *SCM:SH*	
		H 1153	Industries	
–Accidents–Investigation *(May Subd Geog)*	x–x	H 1095	see *SCM:SH*	
–Accounting	x	H 1095	see *SCM:SH*	H 1624
		H 1105	Corp bodies	H 1624
		H 1151.5	Types schools	H 1624
		H 1153	Industries	H 1624
		H 1159	Military srvces	H 1624
–Accounting–Law and legislation *(May Subd Geog)*	x–x	H 1153	Industries	
–Accreditation	x	H 1105	Corp bodies	
–Accreditation *(May Subd Geog)*	x	H 1095	see *SCM:SH*	
		H 1151.5	Types schools	
–Acoustic properties *(May Subd Geog)*	x	H 1149	Chemicals	
		H 1158	Materials	
–Acoustics	x	H 1161	Musical instrum	
–Acquisition	x	H 1154	Languages	
–Acronyms	x	H 1095	see *SCM:SH*	H 1206.5
		H 1154	Languages	H 1206.5
–Acronyms–Dictionaries	x–v	H 1095	see *SCM:SH*	H 1206.5
		H 1154	Languages	H 1206.5
–Acupuncture *(May Subd Geog)*	x	H 1164	Organs of body	

SUBDIVISION	SUBFIELD CODE(S)	FREE-FLOATING LIST IN SCM:SH	CATEGORY	USAGE GUIDELINES IN SCM:SH
–Adaptation *(May Subd Geog)*	x	H 1147 H 1164 H 1180	Animals Organs of body Plants & crops	
–Adaptations	v	H 1110 H 1155.8 H 1156	Indiv pers Lit works/Title Literatures	
–Additives *(May Subd Geog)*	x	H 1158	Materials	
–Address, Forms of	x	H 1154	Languages	
–Adjectivals	x	H 1154	Languages	
–Adjective	x	H 1154	Languages	
–Adjuvant treatment *(May Subd Geog)*	x	H 1150	Diseases	
–Administration	x	H 1095 H 1105 H 1149 H 1149.5 H 1151 H 1151.5	see *SCM:SH* Corp bodies Chemicals Colonies Indiv schools Types schools	
–Administration–Law and legislation *(May Subd Geog)*	x–x	H 1151.5	Types schools	
–Administrative and political divisions	x	H 1140	Places	
–Admission	x	H 1151 H 1151.5	Indiv schools Types schools	
–Admission–Law and legislation *(May Subd Geog)*	x–x	H 1151.5	Types schools	
–Adult education *(May Subd Geog)*	x	H 1187	Christian denom	
–Adverb	x	H 1154	Languages	
–Adverbials	x	H 1154	Languages	
–Adversaries	x	H 1110	Indiv pers	
–Aerial exploration	x	H 1140	Places	

SUBDIVISION	SUBFIELD CODE(S)	FREE-FLOATING LIST IN SCM:SH	CATEGORY	USAGE GUIDELINES IN SCM:SH
–Aerial film and video footage	v	H 1140	Places	
–Aerial gunners	x	H 1159	Military srvces	
–Aerial operations	x	H 1200	Wars	
–Aerial operations, American, [British, etc.]	x	H 1200	Wars	
–Aerial photographs	v	H 1095 H 1140	see SCM:SH Places	H 1210.5
–Aerial views	v	H 1140 H 1151	Places Indiv schools	H 1210.5 H 1210.5
–Aerodynamics	x	H 1195	Land vehicles	
–Aesthetics	x	H 1110 H 1155.2	Indiv pers Groups lit auth	
–Affinity labeling (May Subd Geog)	x	H 1149	Chemicals	
–Affixes	x	H 1154	Languages	
–African American officers	x	H 1159	Military srvces	
–African American troops	x	H 1159	Military srvces	
–African Americans	x	H 1159 H 1200	Military srvces Wars	
–African influences	x	H 1156	Literatures	H 1675
–Age (May Subd Geog)	x	H 1147 H 1180	Animals Plants & crops	
–Age determination (May Subd Geog)	x	H 1147 H 1180	Animals Plants & crops	
–Age factors (May Subd Geog)	x	H 1150	Diseases	
–Aging	x	H 1147 H 1164 H 1180	Animals Organs of body Plants & crops	
–Aging–Genetic aspects	x–x	H 1180	Plants & crops	
–Aging–Molecular aspects	x–x	H 1164	Organs of body	

SUBDIVISION	SUBFIELD CODE(S)	FREE-FLOATING LIST IN SCM:SH	CATEGORY	USAGE GUIDELINES IN SCM:SH
–Aging–Prevention	x	H 1147	Animals	
–Agonists	x	H 1149	Chemicals	
–Agreement	x	H 1154	Languages	
–Agriculture (May Subd Geog)	x	H 1103	Ethnic groups	
–Aides	x	H 1159	Military srvces	
–Air conditioning (May Subd Geog)	x	H 1095 H 1195	see SCM:SH Land vehicles	
–Air conditioning–Control (May Subd Geog)	x	H 1095	see SCM:SH	
–Air content (May Subd Geog)	x	H 1158	Materials	
–Air content–Measurement	x–x	H 1158	Materials	
–Air content–Measurement– Instruments	x–x–x	H 1158	Materials	
–Air disc brakes	x	H 1195	Land vehicles	
–Air police	x	H 1159	Military srvces	
–Air suspension (May Subd Geog)	x	H 1195	Land vehicles	
–Airborne troops	x	H 1159	Military srvces	
–Airborne troops–Communication systems	x–x	H 1159	Military srvces	
–Airmen	x	H 1159	Military srvces	
–Alabama [Illinois, Texas, etc.] delegation	x	H 1155	Legis bodies	
–Alcohol use	x	H 1110	Indiv pers	
–Alcohol use (May Subd Geog)	x	H 1100 H 1103	Classes pers Ethnic groups	
–Algerian authors	x	H 1156	Literatures	
–Allegorical interpretations	x	H 1188	Sacred works	

SUBDIVISION	SUBFIELD CODE(S)	FREE-FLOATING LIST IN SCM:SH	CATEGORY	USAGE GUIDELINES IN SCM:SH
–Allergenicity *(May Subd Geog)*	x	H 1149	Chemicals	
–Allusions	x	H 1110	Indiv pers	
–Alluvial plain	x	H 1145.5	Bodies water	
–Almanacs	v	H 1200	Wars	
–Alphabet	x	H 1154	Languages	
–Alphabet–Religious aspects	x–x	H 1154	Languages	
–Alphabet–Religious aspects– Buddhism, [Christianity, etc.]	x–x–x	H 1154	Languages	
–Alternative treatment *(May Subd Geog)*	x	H 1150	Diseases	
–Altitudes	x	H 1140	Places	
–Alumni and alumnae *(May Subd Geog)*	x	H 1151 H 1151.5	Indiv schools Types schools	
–Amateurs' manuals	v	H 1095	see *SCM:SH*	H 1943.5
–Ambulances	x	H 1159	Military srvces	
–American influences	x	H 1156	Literatures	H 1675
–Amphibious operations	x	H 1200	Wars	
–Analogy	x	H 1154	Languages	
–Analysis	x	H 1095 H 1149 H 1158 H 1180	see *SCM:SH* Chemicals Materials Plants & crops	
–Analysis, appreciation	x	H 1160	Musical comps	
–Anaphora	x	H 1154	Languages	
–Anatomy	x	H 1147 H 1164 H 1180	Animals Organs of body Plants & crops	

SUBDIVISION	SUBFIELD CODE(S)	FREE-FLOATING LIST IN SCM:SH	CATEGORY	USAGE GUIDELINES IN SCM:SH	
–Anecdotes	v	H 1095	see *SCM:SH*		
		H 1100	Classes pers		
		H 1103	Ethnic groups		
		H 1105	Corp bodies		
		H 1110	Indiv pers		
		H 1120	Families		
		H 1140	Places		
		H 1188	Sacred works		
–Animacy	x	H 1154	Languages		
–Animal models *(May Subd Geog)*	x	H 1150	Diseases		
–Ankylosis *(May Subd Geog)*	x	H 1164	Organs of body		
–Annexation to ...	x	H 1140	Places		
–Anniversaries, etc.	x	H 1095	see *SCM:SH*		
		H 1100	Classes pers		
		H 1103	Ethnic groups		
		H 1105	Corp bodies		
		H 1110	Indiv pers		
		H 1140	Places		
		H 1187	Christian denom		
		H 1200	Wars		
–Anodic oxidation *(May Subd Geog)*	x	H 1158	Materials		
–Anonyms and pseudonyms	x	H 1110	Indiv pers		
–Antagonists	x	H 1149	Chemicals		
–Anthropometry *(May Subd Geog)*	x	H 1100	Classes pers		
		H 1103	Ethnic groups		
–Anti-theft devices	x	H 1195	Land vehicles		
–Antiaircraft artillery operations	x	H 1200	Wars		
–Antilock brake systems	x	H 1195	Land vehicles		
–Antiquities	x	H 1103	Ethnic groups	H 1225	
		H 1140	Places	H 1225	H 715
		H 1188	Sacred works		
		H 1200	Wars		

SUBDIVISION	SUBFIELD CODE(S)	FREE-FLOATING LIST IN SCM:SH	CATEGORY	USAGE GUIDELINES IN SCM:SH
–Antiquities–Collection and preservation *(May Subd Geog)*	x–x	H 1103 H 1140	Ethnic groups Places	
–Antiquities–Collectors and collecting *(May Subd Geog)*	x–x	H 1103 H 1140	Ethnic groups Places	
–Antiquities, Byzantine	x	H 1140	Places	H 1225
–Antiquities, Celtic	x	H 1140	Places	H 1225
–Antiquities, Germanic	x	H 1140	Places	H 1225
–Antiquities, Phoenician	x	H 1140	Places	H 1225
–Antiquities, Roman	x	H 1140	Places	H 1225
–Antiquities, Slavic	x	H 1140	Places	H 1225
–Antiquities, Turkish	x	H 1140	Places	H 1225
–Apheresis	x	H 1154	Languages	
–Apologetic works	v	H 1185 H 1187	Religions Christian denom	H 1472 H 1472
–Apologetic works–History and criticism	x–x	H 1185 H 1187	Religions Christian denom	
–Appointments and retirements	x	H 1159	Military srvces	
–Apposition	x	H 1154	Languages	
–Appreciation *(May Subd Geog)*	x	H 1110 H 1148 H 1155.8 H 1156 H 1188	Indiv pers Art Lit works/Title Literatures Sacred works	
–Apprentices	x	H 1159	Military srvces	
–Appropriate technology *(May Subd Geog)*	x	H 1153	Industries	
–Appropriations and expenditures	x	H 1105 H 1140 H 1155 H 1159	Corp bodies Places Legis bodies Military srvces	H 1624 H 1624 H 1624 H 1624

SUBDIVISION	SUBFIELD CODE(S)	FREE-FLOATING LIST IN SCM:SH	CATEGORY	USAGE GUIDELINES IN SCM:SH
–Appropriations and expenditures– Effect of inflation on	x	H 1105 H 1140	Corp bodies Places	
–Arab authors	x	H 1156	Literatures	
–Arab influences	x	H 1156	Literatures	H 1675
–Archaeological collections	x	H 1105 H 1110 H 1120	Corp bodies Indiv pers Families	H 1427 H 1427 H 1427
–Archaisms	x	H 1154	Languages	
–Archival resources	x	H 1095 H 1140	see *SCM:SH* Places	H 1230 H 1230
–Archives	v	H 1095 H 1100 H 1103 H 1105 H 1110 H 1120 H 1151.5 H 1159	see *SCM:SH* Classes pers Ethnic groups Corp bodies Indiv pers Families Types schools Military srvces	H 1230 H 1230 H 1230 H 1230 H 1230 H 1230 H 1230 H 1230
–Archives–Microform catalogs	x–v	H 1095	see *SCM:SH*	
–Area	x	H 1140	Places	
–Armed Forces *(May Subd Geog)*	x	H 1140	Places	
–Armenian authors	x	H 1156	Literatures	
–Armistices	x	H 1200	Wars	
–Armored troops	x	H 1159	Military srvces	
–Art	v	H 1095 H 1110	see *SCM:SH* Indiv pers	H 1250
–Art and the war, [revolution, etc.]	v	H 1200	Wars	
–Art collections	x	H 1105 H 1110 H 1120	Corp bodies Indiv pers Families	H 1427 H 1427 H 1427

SUBDIVISION	SUBFIELD CODE(S)	FREE-FLOATING LIST IN SCM:SH	CATEGORY	USAGE GUIDELINES IN SCM:SH
–Art patronage	x	H 1105 H 1110 H 1120	Corp bodies Indiv pers Families	
–Article	x	H 1154	Languages	
–Artificial insemination *(May Subd Geog)*	x	H 1147	Animals	
–Artificial spawning *(May Subd Geog)*	x	H 1147	Animals	
–Artillery	x	H 1159	Military srvces	
–Artillery–Drill and tactics	x–x	H 1159	Military srvces	
–Artillery operations	x	H 1200	Wars	
–Artillery operations, American, [British, French, etc.]	x	H 1200	Wars	
–Asian Americans	x	H 1159 H 1200	Military srvces Wars	
–Asian authors	x	H 1156	Literatures	
–Asian influences	x	H 1156	Literatures	H 1675
–Aspect	x	H 1154	Languages	
–Aspiration	x	H 1154	Languages	
–Assassination	x	H 1110	Indiv pers	
–Assassination attempt, [date]	x	H 1110	Indiv pers	
–Assassination attempts *(May Subd Geog)*	x x	H 1100 H 1110	Classes pers Indiv pers	
–Assaying *(May Subd Geog)*	x	H 1149	Chemicals	
–Asyndeton	x	H 1154	Languages	
–Atlases	v	H 1095	see *SCM:SH*	H 1935
–Atrocities *(May Subd Geog)*	x	H 1200	Wars	

SUBDIVISION	SUBFIELD CODE(S)	FREE-FLOATING LIST IN SCM:SH	CATEGORY	USAGE GUIDELINES IN SCM:SH
–Attitudes	x	H 1100	Classes pers	H 1955
		H 1103	Ethnic groups	H 1955
–Attribution	x	H 1148	Art	
–Audio adaptations	v	H 1110	Indiv pers	
		H 1156	Literatures	
–Audio equipment *(May Subd Geog)*	x	H 1195	Land vehicles	
–Audio-visual aids	x	H 1095	see *SCM:SH*	H 2110
–Audio-visual aids–Catalogs	x–v	H 1095	see *SCM:SH*	H 1361
–Audiocassette catalogs	v	H 1095	see *SCM:SH*	H 1361
		H 1103	Ethnic groups	H 1361
		H 1105	Corp bodies	H 1361
		H 1110	Indiv pers	H 1361
		H 1140	Places	H 1361
		H 1160	Musical comps	H 1361
–Audiotape catalogs	v	H 1095	see *SCM:SH*	H 1361
		H 1103	Ethnic groups	H 1361
		H 1105	Corp bodies	H 1361
		H 1110	Indiv pers	H 1361
		H 1140	Places	H 1361
		H 1160	Musical comps	H 1361
–Auditing	x	H 1095	see *SCM:SH*	H 1624
		H 1105	Corp bodies	H 1624
		H 1151.5	Types schools	H 1624
		H 1153	Industries	H 1624
–Auditing–Law and legislation *(May Subd Geog)*	x–x	H 1151.5	Types schools	
–Augmentatives	x	H 1154	Languages	
–Australian influences	x	H 1156	Literatures	H 1675
–Authorship	x	H 1095	see *SCM:SH*	
		H 1110	Indiv pers	
		H 1155.8	Lit works/Title	
		H 1188	Sacred works	
–Authorship–Collaboration	x–x	H 1110	Indiv pers	
–Authorship–Date of authorship	x–x	H 1188	Sacred works	

SUBDIVISION	SUBFIELD CODE(S)	FREE-FLOATING LIST IN SCM:SH	CATEGORY	USAGE GUIDELINES IN SCM:SH
–Authorship–Style manuals	x-v	H 1095	see *SCM:SH*	
–Autographs	v	H 1100	Classes pers	
		H 1103	Ethnic groups	
		H 1110	Indiv pers	
		H 1200	Wars	
–Automatic control	x	H 1095	see *SCM:SH*	
		H 1195	Land vehicles	
–Automation	x	H 1095	see *SCM:SH*	
		H 1105	Corp bodies	
		H 1153	Industries	
–Autonomous communities	x	H 1095	see *SCM:SH*	H 713
–Autonomous regions	x	H 1095	see *SCM:SH*	H 713
–Autopsy *(May Subd Geog)*	x	H 1147	Animals	
–Auxiliary verbs	x	H 1154	Languages	
–Aviation	x	H 1159	Military srvces	
–Aviation–Ground support	x–x	H 1159	Military srvces	
–Aviation–Job descriptions	x–v	H 1159	Military srvces	
–Aviation electronics technicians	x	H 1159	Military srvces	
–Aviation mechanics	x	H 1159	Military srvces	
–Aviation supplies and stores	x	H 1159	Military srvces	
–Awards	x	H 1105	Corp bodies	
		H 1110	Indiv pers	
		H 1159	Military srvces	
–Awards *(May Subd Geog)*	x	H 1095	see *SCM:SH*	
–Axles	x	H 1195	Land vehicles	
–Bahai interpretations	x	H 1188	Sacred works	
–Balloons *(May Subd Geog)*	x	H 1200	Wars	
–Bandmasters	x	H 1159	Military srvces	

SUBDIVISION	SUBFIELD CODE(S)	FREE-FLOATING LIST IN SCM:SH	CATEGORY	USAGE GUIDELINES IN SCM:SH
–Bands	x	H 1151	Indiv schools	
–Bangladeshi authors	x	H 1156	Literatures	
–Barracks and quarters	x	H 1159	Military srvces	
–Barracks and quarters–Furniture	x–x	H 1159	Military srvces	
–Barrier-free design *(May Subd Geog)*	x	H 1095	see *SCM:SH*	
–Baseball	x	H 1151	Indiv schools	
–Basketball	x	H 1151	Indiv schools	
–Basque authors	x	H 1156	Literatures	
–Basques *(May Subd Geog)*	x	H 1200	Wars	
–Bathymetric maps	v	H 1140	Places	
–Batteries *(May Subd Geog)*	x	H 1195	Land vehicles	
–Battlefields *(May Subd Geog)*	x	H 1200	Wars	
–Bearings *(May Subd Geog)*	x	H 1195	Land vehicles	
–Behavior *(May Subd Geog)*	x	H 1147	Animals	
–Behavior–Climatic factors *(May Subd Geog)*	x–x	H 1147	Animals	
–Behavior–Endocrine aspects	x–x	H 1147	Animals	
–Behavior–Evolution *(May Subd Geog)*	x–x	H 1147	Animals	
–Benefactors	x	H 1151	Indiv schools	
–Benefices *(May Subd Geog)*	x	H 1187	Christian denom	
–Bengali authors	x	H 1156	Literatures	
–Biblical teaching	x	H 1095	see *SCM:SH*	H 1295
–Bibliography	v	H 1095	see *SCM:SH*	
		H 1156	Literatures	
		H 1160	Musical comps	

SUBDIVISION	SUBFIELD CODE(S)	FREE-FLOATING LIST IN SCM:SH	CATEGORY	USAGE GUIDELINES IN SCM:SH	
–Bibliography–Catalogs	v–v	H 1095	see *SCM:SH*	H 1361	
–Bibliography–Early	v–v	H 1095	see *SCM:SH*	H 1576	
–Bibliography–Exhibitions	v–v	H 1095	see *SCM:SH*	H 1593	
–Bibliography–Graded lists	v–v	H 1160	Musical comps		
–Bibliography–Methodology	x–x	H 1095	see *SCM:SH*		
–Bibliography–Microform catalogs	v–v	H 1095	see *SCM:SH*	H 1361	H 1965
–Bibliography–Union lists	v–v	H 1095	see *SCM:SH*	H 1361	
–Bibliography of bibliographies	v	H 1095	see *SCM:SH*		
–Bio-bibliography	v	H 1095	see *SCM:SH*	H 1328	
		H 1103	Ethnic groups	H 1328	
		H 1140	Places	H 1328	
		H 1186	Relig orders	H 1328	
		H 1187	Christian denom	H 1328	
–Bioaccumulation *(May Subd Geog)*	x	H 1149	Chemicals		
–Bioavailability *(May Subd Geog)*	x	H 1149	Chemicals		
–Biocompatibility *(May Subd Geog)*	x	H 1158	Materials		
–Biodegradation *(May Subd Geog)*	x	H 1149	Chemicals		
		H 1158	Materials		
–Biography	v	H 1095	see *SCM:SH*	H 1330	
		H 1100	Classes pers	H 1330	
		H 1103	Ethnic groups	H 1330	
		H 1105	Corp bodies	H 1330	
		H 1140	Places	H 1330	H 1845
		H 1147	Animals	H 1330	H 1720
		H 1159	Military srvces	H 1330	
		H 1188	Sacred works	H 1330	
		H 1200	Wars	H 1330	
–Biography–Anecdotes	v–v	H 1140	Places		
–Biography–Caricatures and cartoons	v–v	H 1140	Places		

SUBDIVISION	SUBFIELD CODE(S)	FREE-FLOATING LIST IN SCM:SH	CATEGORY	USAGE GUIDELINES IN SCM:SH
–Biography–Dictionaries	v–v	H 1095	see *SCM:SH*	
		H 1100	Classes pers	
		H 1103	Ethnic groups	
		H 1105	Corp bodies	
		H 1140	Places	
–Biography–History and criticism	x–x	H 1095	see *SCM:SH*	
		H 1100	Classes pers	
		H 1103	Ethnic groups	
		H 1105	Corp bodies	
		H 1140	Places	
–Biography–Humor	v–v	H 1140	Places	
–Biography–Pictorial works	v–v	H 1100	Classes pers	
		H 1103	Ethnic groups	
		H 1140	Places	
–Biography–Portraits	v–v	H 1105	Corp bodies	
		H 1140	Places	
		H 1159	Military srvces	
–Biography–Sermons	v–v	H 1188	Sacred works	
–Biography–Sources	x–v	H 1100	Classes pers	
		H 1103	Ethnic groups	
		H 1140	Places	
–Biological control *(May Subd Geog)*	x	H 1147	Animals	
		H 1180	Plants & crops	
–Biological warfare *(May Subd Geog)*	x	H 1200	Wars	
–Biopsy *(May Subd Geog)*	x	H 1164	Organs of body	
–Biotechnology *(May Subd Geog)*	x	H 1149	Chemicals	
		H 1180	Plants & crops	
–Birth	x	H 1110	Indiv pers	
–Birthplace	x	H 1110	Indiv pers	
–Bishops	x	H 1187	Christian denom	
–Bishops–Appointment, call, and election	x–x	H 1187	Christian denom	
–Black authors	x	H 1156	Literatures	

SUBDIVISION	SUBFIELD CODE(S)	FREE-FLOATING LIST IN SCM:SH	CATEGORY	USAGE GUIDELINES IN SCM:SH
–Black interpretations	x	H 1188	Sacred works	
–Blacks *(May Subd Geog)*	x	H 1200	Wars	
–Blockades *(May Subd Geog)*	x	H 1200	Wars	
–Blogs *(May Subd Geog)*	v	H 1095	see *SCM:SH*	
		H 1100	Classes pers	
		H 1103	Ethnic groups	
		H 1110	Indiv pers	
–Blood-vessels	x	H 1164	Organs of body	
–Blunt trauma *(May Subd Geog)*	x	H 1164	Organs of body	
–Boats	x	H 1159	Military srvces	
–Boats *(May Subd Geog)*	x	H 1103	Ethnic groups	
–Boatswain's mates	x	H 1159	Military srvces	
–Boatswains	x	H 1159	Military srvces	
–Bodies *(May Subd Geog)*	x	H 1195	Land vehicles	
–Bodies–Alignment *(May Subd Geog)*	x–x	H 1195	Land vehicles	
–Bodies–Parts *(May Subd Geog)*	x–x	H 1195	Land vehicles	
–Boiler technicians	x	H 1159	Military srvces	
–Bomb reconnaissance	x	H 1200	Wars	
–Bonding *(May Subd Geog)*	x	H 1100	Classes pers	
–Boning *(May Subd Geog)*	x	H 1147	Animals	
–Bonsai collections	x	H 1105	Corp bodies	H 1427
		H 1110	Indiv pers	H 1427
		H 1120	Families	H 1427
–Book reviews	v	H 1095	see *SCM:SH*	H 2021
		H 1100	Classes pers	H 2021
		H 1103	Ethnic groups	H 2021
		H 1140	Places	H 2021
–Books and reading	x	H 1110	Indiv pers	H 1333

SUBDIVISION	SUBFIELD CODE(S)	FREE-FLOATING LIST IN SCM:SH	CATEGORY	USAGE GUIDELINES IN SCM:SH	
–Books and reading *(May Subd Geog)*	x	H 1100 H 1103	Classes pers Ethnic groups	H 1333 H 1333	
–Boundaries *(May Subd Geog)*	x	H 1140 H 1149.5	Places Colonies	H 1333.5 H 1333.5	
–Bowing	x	H 1161	Musical instrum		
–Brakes	x	H 1195	Land vehicles		
–Brazilian influences	x	H 1156	Literatures	H 1675	
–Brazing *(May Subd Geog)*	x	H 1149	Chemicals		
–Breaking in	x	H 1195	Land vehicles		
–Breath control	x	H 1161	Musical instrum		
–Breeding *(May Subd Geog)*	x	H 1147 H 1180	Animals Plants & crops		
–Breeding–Selection indexes	x–x	H 1147	Animals		
–Brittleness *(May Subd Geog)*	x	H 1149 H 1158	Chemicals Materials		
–Buddhist authors	x	H 1156	Literatures		
–Buddhist influences	x	H 1156	Literatures	H 1675	
–Buddhist interpretations	x	H 1188	Sacred works		
–Buildings	x	H 1095 H 1105 H 1151	see *SCM:SH* Corp bodies Indiv schools		
–Buildings–Barrier-free design	x–x	H 1151	Indiv schools		
–Buildings, structures, etc.	x	H 1140	Places	H 832	H 1334
–Buildings, structures, etc.– Conservation and restoration	x	H 1140	Places		
–Bumpers	x	H 1195	Land vehicles		
–Business management	x	H 1151.5	Types schools		

SUBDIVISION	SUBFIELD CODE(S)	FREE-FLOATING LIST IN SCM:SH	CATEGORY	USAGE GUIDELINES IN SCM:SH
–By-laws	v	H 1095 H 1105	see *SCM:SH* Corp bodies	
–By-products	x	H 1095	see *SCM:SH*	
–Cadenzas	v	H 1160	Musical comps	
–Calcification *(May Subd Geog)*	x	H 1164	Organs of body	
–Calendars	v	H 1095 H 1105 H 1110 H 1140	see *SCM:SH* Corp bodies Indiv pers Places	
–Calibration *(May Subd Geog)*	x	H 1095	see *SCM:SH*	
–Camouflage	x	H 1200	Wars	
–Campaigns *(May Subd Geog)*	x	H 1200	Wars	H 1285
–Cancer *(May Subd Geog)*	x	H 1164	Organs of body	
–Cannibalism *(May Subd Geog)*	x	H 1147	Animals	
–Canon	x	H 1188	Sacred works	
–Canonical criticism	x	H 1188	Sacred works	
–Cantons	x	H 1095	see *SCM:SH*	H 713
–Capital and capitol	x	H 1140	Places	
–Capital investments *(May Subd Geog)*	x	H 1153	Industries	
–Capital productivity *(May Subd Geog)*	x	H 1153	Industries	
–Capitalization	x	H 1154	Languages	
–Captivity, [dates]	x	H 1110	Indiv pers	
–Carbon content *(May Subd Geog)*	x	H 1158	Materials	
–Carcasses *(May Subd Geog)*	x	H 1147	Animals	
–Carcasses–Biodegradation *(May Subd Geog)*	x–x	H 1147	Animals	

SUBDIVISION	SUBFIELD CODE(S)	FREE-FLOATING LIST IN SCM:SH	CATEGORY	USAGE GUIDELINES IN SCM:SH
–Carcasses–Grading *(May Subd Geog)*	x–x	H 1147	Animals	
–Carcasses–Handling *(May Subd Geog)*	x–x	H 1147	Animals	
–Carcinogenicity *(May Subd Geog)*	x	H 1149	Chemicals	
–Cardiovascular system	x	H 1147	Animals	
–Care *(May Subd Geog)*	x	H 1100	Classes pers	
–Care and hygiene *(May Subd Geog)*	x	H 1164	Organs of body	
–Career in [specific field or discipline]	x	H 1110	Indiv pers	
–Caribbean authors	x	H 1156	Literatures	
–Caricatures and cartoons	v	H 1095	see *SCM:SH*	
		H 1100	Classes pers	
		H 1103	Ethnic groups	
		H 1105	Corp bodies	
		H 1110	Indiv pers	
		H 1120	Families	
		H 1188	Sacred works	
–Cartography	x	H 1200	Wars	
–Case	x	H 1154	Languages	
–Case grammar	x	H 1154	Languages	
–Case studies	v	H 1095	see *SCM:SH*	H 1350
		H 1100	Classes pers	H 1350
		H 1103	Ethnic groups	H 1350
		H 1105	Corp bodies	H 1350
–Cases	v	H 1154.5	Legal topics	H 1350
–Casualties *(May Subd Geog)*	x	H 1200	Wars	
–Casualties–Statistics	x–v	H 1200	Wars	H 2095
–Catalan authors	x	H 1156	Literatures	

SUBDIVISION	SUBFIELD CODE(S)	FREE-FLOATING LIST IN SCM:SH	CATEGORY	USAGE GUIDELINES IN SCM:SH	
–Catalogs	v	H 1095	see *SCM:SH*	H 1360	H 1361
		H 1105	Corp bodies	H 1360	H 1361
		H 1110	Indiv pers	H 1360	H 1361
		H 1120	Families	H 1360	H 1361
		H 1148	Art	H 1360	
–Catalogs, Manufacturers'	v	H 1161	Musical instrum		
–Catalogs and collections *(May Subd Geog)*	v	H 1095	see *SCM:SH*	H 1360	H 1427
		H 1147	Animals	H 1360	H 1427
		H 1161	Musical instrum	H 1360	H 1427
		H 1180	Plants & crops	H 1360	H 1427
–Catalogues raisonnés	v	H 1110	Indiv pers		
–Catalytic converters	x	H 1195	Land vehicles		
–Cataphora	x	H 1154	Languages		
–Catechisms	v	H 1185	Religions		
		H 1187	Christian denom		
–Catechisms–English, [French, German, etc.]	v–x	H 1187	Christian denom		
–Catechisms–History and criticism	x–x	H 1187	Christian denom		
–Categorial grammar	x	H 1154	Languages		
–Catholic authors	x	H 1156	Literatures		
–Caucuses	x	H 1155	Legis bodies		
–Causative	x	H 1154	Languages		
–Causes	x	H 1200	Wars		
–Cavalry	x	H 1159	Military srvces		
–Cavalry–Drill and tactics	x–x	H 1159	Military srvces		
–Cavalry operations	x	H 1200	Wars		
–Cavitation erosion *(May Subd Geog)*	x	H 1158	Materials		
–CD-ROM catalogs	v	H 1095	see *SCM:SH*	H 1361	

SUBDIVISION	SUBFIELD CODE(S)	FREE-FLOATING LIST IN SCM:SH	CATEGORY	USAGE GUIDELINES IN SCM:SH
–Celtic authors	x	H 1156	Literatures	
–Celtic influences	x	H 1156	Literatures	H 1675
–Censorship *(May Subd Geog)*	x	H 1095 H 1110 H 1156 H 1200	see *SCM:SH* Indiv persons Literatures Wars	
–Censures	x	H 1110 H 1155	Indiv pers Legis bodies	
–Census	v	H 1103 H 1140	Ethnic groups Places	H 1366 H 1366
–Census–Law and legislation	x–x	H 1140	Places	
–Census, [date]	v	H 1103 H 1140	Ethnic groups Places	H 1366 H 1366
–Centennial celebrations, etc.	x	H 1095 H 1105 H 1140 H 1200	see *SCM:SH* Corp bodies Places Wars	
–Certification *(May Subd Geog)*	x	H 1095 H 1100 H 1153	see *SCM:SH* Classes pers Industries	
–Channelization	x	H 1145.5	Bodies water	
–Channels	x	H 1145.5	Bodies water	
–Chapel exercises	v	H 1151.5	Types schools	
–Chaplain's assistants	x	H 1159	Military srvces	
–Chaplains	x	H 1105 H 1159	Corp bodies Military srvces	
–Chaplains *(May Subd Geog)*	x	H 1200	Wars	
–Characters	x	H 1110 H 1155.8	Indiv pers Lit works/Title	
–Characters–Children, [Jews, Physicians, etc.]	x	H 1110	Indiv pers	

SUBDIVISION	SUBFIELD CODE(S)	FREE-FLOATING LIST IN SCM:SH	CATEGORY	USAGE GUIDELINES IN SCM:SH
–Characters–[name of individual character]	x–x	H 1110	Indiv pers	
–Charitable contributions *(May Subd Geog)*	x	H 1095	see *SCM:SH*	
		H 1100	Classes pers	
		H 1103	Ethnic groups	
–Charities	x	H 1103	Ethnic groups	
		H 1105	Corp bodies	
		H 1185	Religions	
		H 1187	Christian denom	
–Charters	v	H 1105	Corp bodies	
		H 1140	Places	
–Charters, grants, privileges	v	H 1140	Places	
–Charts, diagrams, etc.	v	H 1095	see *SCM:SH*	
–Chassis	x	H 1195	Land vehicles	
–Chemical defenses *(May Subd Geog)*	x	H 1147	Animals	
		H 1180	Plants & crops	
–Chemical resistance	x	H 1158	Materials	
–Chemical warfare *(May Subd Geog)*	x	H 1200	Wars	
–Chemoprevention *(May Subd Geog)*	x	H 1150	Diseases	
–Chemotaxonomy *(May Subd Geog)*	x	H 1180	Plants & crops	
–Chemotherapy *(May Subd Geog)*	x	H 1150	Diseases	
–Chemotherapy–Complications *(May Subd Geog)*	x–x	H 1150	Diseases	
–Childhood and youth	x	H 1110	Indiv pers	
–Children *(May Subd Geog)*	x	H 1200	Wars	
–Children's sermons	v	H 1188	Sacred works	
–Children's use *(May Subd Geog)*	x	H 1188	Sacred works	
–Chinese authors	x	H 1156	Literatures	
–Chinese influences	x	H 1156	Literatures	H 1675

SUBDIVISION	SUBFIELD CODE(S)	FREE-FLOATING LIST IN SCM:SH	CATEGORY	USAGE GUIDELINES IN SCM:SH
–Chiropractic treatment *(May Subd Geog)*	x	H 1150	Diseases	
–Choral organizations	x	H 1151	Indiv schools	
–Chord diagrams	v	H 1161	Musical instrum	
–Chorus scores with organ	v	H 1160	Musical comps	
–Chorus scores with piano	v	H 1160	Musical comps	
–Chorus scores without accompaniment	v	H 1160	Musical comps	
–Chosŏn dynasty, 1392-1910	y	H 1148	Korean art	
–Christian authors	x	H 1156	Literatures	
–Christian influences	x	H 1156	Literatures	H 1675
–Christian Science authors	x	H 1156	Literatures	
–Chronology	v	H 1095	see *SCM:SH*	H 1367
		H 1110	Indiv pers	H 1367
		H 1148	Art	H 1367
		H 1155.2	Groups lit auth	H 1367
		H 1156	Literatures	H 1367
		H 1188	Sacred works	H 1367
		H 1200	Wars	H 1367
–Church history	x	H 1140	Places	
–Church history–16th century	x–y	H 1140	Places	
–Church history–17th century	x–y	H 1140	Places	
–Church history–18th century	x–y	H 1140	Places	
–Church history–19th century	x–y	H 1140	Places	
–Church history–20th century	x–y	H 1140	Places	
–Church history–21st century	x–y	H 1140	Places	
–Cipher	x	H 1110	Indiv pers	
–Circulation	x	H 1095	see *SCM:SH*	

SUBDIVISION	SUBFIELD CODE(S)	FREE-FLOATING LIST IN SCM:SH	CATEGORY	USAGE GUIDELINES IN SCM:SH	
–Citizen participation	x	H 1095	see *SCM:SH*	H 1942	
–Civic action	x	H 1159	Military srvces		
–Civil functions	x	H 1159	Military srvces		
–Civil rights *(May Subd Geog)*	x	H 1100 H 1103	Classes pers Ethnic groups		
–Civilian employees	x	H 1159	Military srvces		
–Civilian relief *(May Subd Geog)*	x	H 1200	Wars		
–Civilization	x	H 1140	Places	H 1370	
–Civilization–16th century	x–y	H 1140	Places	H 1370	
–Civilization–17th century	x–y	H 1140	Places	H 1370	
–Civilization–18th century	x–y	H 1140	Places	H 1370	
–Civilization–19th century	x–y	H 1140	Places	H 1370	
–Civilization–20th century	x–y	H 1140	Places	H 1370	
–Civilization–21st century	x–y	H 1140	Places	H 1370	
–Civilization–Foreign influences	x–x	H 1140	Places	H 1370	H 1675
–Civilization–Philosophy	x–x	H 1140	Places		
–Cladistic analysis *(May Subd Geog)*	x	H 1095	Plants & crops		
–Claims	x	H 1103 H 1140 H 1200	Ethnic groups Places Wars		
–Claims vs. ...	x	H 1105 H 1110 H 1140	Corp bodies Indiv pers Places		
–Classical influences	x	H 1156	Literatures	H 1675	
–Classification	v	H 1095 H 1100 H 1147 H 1154 H 1180	see *SCM:SH* Classes pers Animals Languages Plants & crops		

SUBDIVISION	SUBFIELD CODE(S)	FREE-FLOATING LIST IN SCM:SH	CATEGORY	USAGE GUIDELINES IN SCM:SH
–Classification–Molecular aspects	x–x	H 1147 H 1180	Animals Plants & crops	
–Classifiers	x	H 1154	Languages	
–Clauses	x	H 1154	Languages	
–Cleaning *(May Subd Geog)*	x	H 1095	see *SCM:SH*	
–Clergy	x	H 1187	Christian denom	
–Clergy–Appointment, call and election	x–x	H 1187	Christian denom	
–Clergy–Degradation	x–x	H 1187	Christian denom	
–Clergy–Deposition	x–x	H 1187	Christian denom	
–Clergy–Deprivation of the clerical garb *(May Subd Geog)*	x–x	H 1187	Christian denom	
–Clergy–Installation *(May Subd Geog)*	x–x	H 1187	Christian denom	
–Clergy–Secular employment *(May Subd Geog)*	x–x	H 1187	Christian denom	
–Clerical work	x	H 1159	Military srvces	
–Climate	x	H 1140	Places	
–Climate–Observations	x–v	H 1140	Places	
–Climatic factors *(May Subd Geog)*	x	H 1147 H 1180 H 1195	Animals Plants & crops Land vehicles	
–Clitics	x	H 1154	Languages	
–Clones *(May Subd Geog)*	x	H 1180	Plants & crops	
–Clones–Selection *(May Subd Geog)*	x–x	H 1180	Plants & crops	
–Clones–Variation *(May Subd Geog)*	x–x	H 1180	Plants & crops	
–Cloning *(May Subd Geog)*	x	H 1147	Animals	

SUBDIVISION	SUBFIELD CODE(S)	FREE-FLOATING LIST IN SCM:SH	CATEGORY	USAGE GUIDELINES IN SCM:SH
–Clothing	x	H 1110 H 1120	Indiv pers Families	
–Clothing *(May Subd Geog)*	x	H 1100 H 1103	Classes pers Ethnic groups	
–Cloture	x	H 1155	Legis bodies	
–Clutches *(May Subd Geog)*	x	H 1195	Land vehicles	
–Cobalt content *(May Subd Geog)*	x	H 1158	Materials	
–Code numbers	v	H 1095	see *SCM:SH*	
–Code words	v	H 1095	see *SCM:SH*	
–Codification	x	H 1154.5	Legal topics	
–Cognate words	x	H 1154	Languages	
–Cognate words–Dutch, [German, etc.]	x–x	H 1154	Languages	
–Coin collections	x	H 1105 H 1110 H 1120	Corp bodies Indiv pers Families	H 1427 H 1427 H 1427
–Cold weather conditions	x	H 1095	see *SCM:SH*	
–Cold weather operation *(May Subd Geog)*	x	H 1195	Land vehicles	
–Cold working *(May Subd Geog)*	x	H 1149 H 1158	Chemicals Materials	
–Collaborationists *(May Subd Geog)*	x	H 1200	Wars	
–Collectibles *(May Subd Geog)*	x	H 1095 H 1100 H 1103 H 1105 H 1110 H 1200	see *SCM:SH* Classes pers Ethnic groups Corp bodies Indiv pers Wars	
–Collection and preservation *(May Subd Geog)*	x	H 1095 H 1147 H 1180	see *SCM:SH* Animals Plants & crops	

SUBDIVISION	SUBFIELD CODE(S)	FREE-FLOATING LIST IN SCM:SH	CATEGORY	USAGE GUIDELINES IN SCM:SH
–Collective nouns	x	H 1154	Languages	
–Collectors and collecting *(May Subd Geog)*	x	H 1095 H 1195	see *SCM:SH* Land vehicles	
–Collectors and collecting–Taxation *(May Subd Geog)*	x–x	H 1195	Land vehicles	
–Collectors and collecting–Taxation–Law and legislation *(May Subd Geog)*	x–x	H 1195	Land vehicles	
–Collier service	x	H 1159	Military srvces	
–Collision avoidance systems *(May Subd Geog)*	x	H 1195	Land vehicles	
–Collision damage *(May Subd Geog)*	x	H 1195	Land vehicles	
–Colonial forces *(May Subd Geog)*	x	H 1159	Military srvces	
–Colonial influence	x	H 1140	Places	
–Colonies	x	H 1095 H 1140	see *SCM:SH* Places	
–Colonization	x	H 1140	Places	
–Colonization *(May Subd Geog)*	x	H 1100 H 1103 H 1147 H 1180	Classes pers Ethnic groups Animals Plants & crops	
–Color *(May Subd Geog)*	x	H 1147 H 1180	Animals Plants & crops	
–Color–Fading *(May Subd Geog)*	x–x	H 1180	Plants & crops	
–Color–Fading–Control *(May Subd Geog)*	x–x–x	H 1180	Plants & crops	
–Color–Genetic aspects	x–x	H 1180	Plants & crops	
–Coloring	x	H 1149 H 1158	Chemicals Materials	
–Combat sustainability	x	H 1159	Military srvces	

SUBDIVISION	SUBFIELD CODE(S)	FREE-FLOATING LIST IN SCM:SH	CATEGORY	USAGE GUIDELINES IN SCM:SH
–Combustion *(May Subd Geog)*	x	H 1158	Materials	
–Comedies	x	H 1110	Indiv pers	
–Comic books, strips, etc.	v	H 1095	see *SCM:SH*	
		H 1100	Classes pers	
		H 1103	Ethnic groups	
		H 1105	Corp bodies	
		H 1110	Indiv pers	
		H 1188	Sacred works	
–Commando operations *(May Subd Geog)*	x	H 1200	Wars	
–Commando troops	x	H 1159	Military srvces	
–Commentaries	v	H 1188	Sacred works	
–Commentaries–History and criticism	x–x	H 1188	Sacred works	
–Commerce *(May Subd Geog)*	x	H 1103	Ethnic groups	
		H 1140	Places	
		H 1149.5	Colonies	
–Commercial policy	x	H 1140	Places	
–Commercial treaties	v	H 1140	Places	H 2227
–Commissariat	x	H 1159	Military srvces	
–Committees	x	H 1155	Legis bodies	
–Committees–Indexes	x–v	H 1155	Legis bodies	
–Committees–Rules and practice	x–v	H 1155	Legis bodies	
–Committees–Seniority system	x	H 1155	Legis bodies	
–Communication	x	H 1103	Ethnic groups	
–Communication systems	x	H 1095	see *SCM:SH*	
		H 1105	Corp bodies	
		H 1151.5	Types schools	
		H 1153	Industries	
		H 1159	Military srvces	

SUBDIVISION	SUBFIELD CODE(S)	FREE-FLOATING LIST IN SCM:SH	CATEGORY	USAGE GUIDELINES IN SCM:SH
–Communication systems– Contracting out *(May Subd Geog)*	x–x	H 1151.5	Types schools	
–Communications	x	H 1200	Wars	
–Compact disc catalogs	v	H 1095	see *SCM:SH*	H 1361
		H 1105	Corp bodies	H 1361
		H 1110	Indiv persons	H 1361
		H 1140	Places	H 1361
–Comparative clauses	x	H 1154	Languages	
–Comparative method	x	H 1095	see *SCM:SH*	
–Comparative studies	v	H 1095	see *SCM:SH*	
		H 1187	Christian denom	
		H 1188	Sacred works	
–Comparison	x	H 1154	Languages	
–Competitions *(May Subd Geog)*	x	H 1095	see *SCM:SH*	
–Complaints against *(May Subd Geog)*	x	H 1151.5	Types schools	
–Complement	x	H 1154	Languages	
–Compliance costs *(May Subd Geog)*	x	H 1154.5	Legal topics	
–Complications *(May Subd Geog)*	x	H 1150	Diseases	
–Composition	x	H 1095	see *SCM:SH*	
		H 1147	Animals	
		H 1180	Plants & crops	
–Composition and exercises	x	H 1154	Languages	
–Compound words	x	H 1154	Languages	
–Compression testing *(May Subd Geog)*	x	H 1158	Materials	
–Computer-aided design *(May Subd Geog)*	x	H 1095	see *SCM:SH*	
–Computer-assisted instruction	x	H 1095	see *SCM:SH*	
		H 1154	Languages	

SUBDIVISION	SUBFIELD CODE(S)	FREE-FLOATING LIST IN SCM:SH	CATEGORY	USAGE GUIDELINES IN SCM:SH
–Computer-assisted instruction for foreign speakers	x	H 1154	Languages	
–Computer-assisted instruction for French, [Spanish, etc.] speakers	x	H 1154	Languages	
–Computer games	v	H 1095	see *SCM:SH*	
–Computer network resources	x	H 1095	see *SCM:SH*	
–Computer networks *(May Subd Geog)*	x	H 1095	see *SCM:SH*	
–Computer networks–Security measures *(May Subd Geog)*	x–x	H 1095	see *SCM:SH*	
–Computer programs	x	H 1095	see *SCM:SH*	H 2070
–Computer simulation	x	H 1095	see *SCM:SH*	H 2040
–Concentration camps *(May Subd Geog)*	x	H 1200	Wars	
–Concessive clauses	x	H 1154	Languages	
–Concordances	v	H 1095	see *SCM:SH*	H 1670
		H 1110	Indiv pers	H 1670
		H 1156	Literatures	H 1670
		H 1188	Sacred works	H 1670
–Concordances, English	v	H 1188	Sacred works	
–Concordances, English–Authorized, [Living Bible, Revised Standard, etc.]	v–x	H 1188	Sacred works	
–Concordances, French, [German, etc.]	v	H 1188	Sacred works	
–Condition scoring *(May Subd Geog)*	x	H 1147	Animals	
–Conditionals	x	H 1154	Languages	
–Conduct of life	x	H 1100	Classes pers	
–Conference committees	x	H 1155	Legis bodies	

SUBDIVISION	SUBFIELD CODE(S)	FREE-FLOATING LIST IN SCM:SH	CATEGORY	USAGE GUIDELINES IN SCM:SH
–Confiscations and contributions (May Subd Geog)	x	H 1200	Wars	
–Conformation	x	H 1149	Chemicals	
–Conformation (May Subd Geog)	x	H 1147	Animals	
–Confucian influences	x	H 1156	Literatures	
–Congresses	v	H 1095	see SCM:SH	H 1460
–Congresses–Attendance	x–x	H 1095	see SCM:SH	
–Conjunctions	x	H 1154	Languages	
–Connectives	x	H 1154	Languages	
–Conscientious objectors (May Subd Geog)	x	H 1200	Wars	
–Conscript labor (May Subd Geog)	x	H 1200	Wars	
–Conservation (May Subd Geog)	x	H 1147 H 1158 H 1180	Animals Materials Plants & crops	
–Conservation–Law and legislation (May Subd Geog)	x–x	H 1147 H 1180	Animals Plants & crops	
–Conservation and restoration (May Subd Geog)	x	H 1095 H 1148 H 1195	see SCM:SH Art Land vehicles	
–Conservation and restoration– Taxation (May Subd Geog)	x	H 1195	Land vehicles	
–Conservation and restoration– Taxation–Law and legislation (May Subd Geog)	x	H 1195	Land vehicles	
–Consonants	x	H 1154	Languages	
–Constituent communication	x	H 1155	Legis bodies	
–Constitution	v	H 1105	Corp bodies	
–Construction (May Subd Geog)	x	H 1161	Musical instrum	

SUBDIVISION	SUBFIELD CODE(S)	FREE-FLOATING LIST IN SCM:SH	CATEGORY	USAGE GUIDELINES IN SCM:SH
–Construction mechanics	x	H 1159	Military srvces	
–Contemporaries	x	H 1110	Indiv pers	
–Contested elections	x	H 1155	Legis bodies	
–Context	x	H 1154	Languages	
–Contraction	x	H 1154	Languages	
–Contraction *(May Subd Geog)*	x	H 1164	Organs of body	
–Control *(May Subd Geog)*	x	H 1095 H 1147 H 1180	see *SCM:SH* Animals Plants & crops	
–Control–Environmental aspects *(May Subd Geog)*	x–x	H 1147 H 1180	Animals Plants & crops	
–Control–Law and legislation *(May Subd Geog)*	x–x	H 1147 H 1180	Animals Plants & crops	
–Controlled release *(May Subd Geog)*	x	H 1149	Chemicals	
–Controversial literature	v	H 1185 H 1186 H 1187 H 1188	Religions Relig orders Christian denom Sacred works	H 1472 H 1472 H 1472 H 1472
–Controversial literature–History and criticism	x–x	H 1185 H 1186 H 1187 H 1188	Religions Relig orders Christian denom Sacred works	
–Conversation and phrase books	v	H 1154	Languages	
–Conversation and phrase books–English	v–x	H 1154	Languages	
–Conversation and phrase books–French, [Italian, etc.]	v–x	H 1154	Languages	
–Conversation and phrase books–Polyglot	v–x	H 1154	Languages	
–Conversation and phrase books (for accountants)	v	H 1154	Languages	

SUBDIVISION	SUBFIELD CODE(S)	FREE-FLOATING LIST IN SCM:SH	CATEGORY	USAGE GUIDELINES IN SCM:SH
–Conversation and phrase books (for air pilots)	v	H 1154	Languages	
–Conversation and phrase books (for animal specialists)	v	H 1154	Languages	
–Conversation and phrase books (for bank employees)	v	H 1154	Languages	
–Conversation and phrase books (for businesspeople)	v	H 1154	Languages	
–Conversation and phrase books (for caregivers)	v	H 1154	Languages	
–Conversation and phrase books (for clergy, etc.)	v	H 1154	Languages	
–Conversation and phrase books (for computer industry employees)	v	H 1154	Languages	
–Conversation and phrase books (for construction industry employees)	v	H 1154	Languages	
–Conversation and phrase books (for correctional personnel)	v	H 1154	Languages	
–Conversation and phrase books (for dental personnel)	v	H 1154	Languages	
–Conversation and phrase books (for diplomats)	v	H 1154	Languages	
–Conversation and phrase books (for domestics)	v	H 1154	Languages	
–Conversation and phrase books (for farmers)	v	H 1154	Languages	
–Conversation and phrase books (for fire fighters)	v	H 1154	Languages	
–Conversation and phrase books (for first responders)	v	H 1154	Languages	

SUBDIVISION	SUBFIELD CODE(S)	FREE-FLOATING LIST IN SCM:SH	CATEGORY	USAGE GUIDELINES IN SCM:SH
–Conversation and phrase books (for fishers)	v	H 1154	Languages	
–Conversation and phrase books (for flight attendants)	v	H 1154	Languages	
–Conversation and phrase books (for gardeners)	v	H 1154	Languages	
–Conversation and phrase books (for geologists)	v	H 1154	Languages	
–Conversation and phrase books (for gourmets)	v	H 1154	Languages	
–Conversation and phrase books (for homeowners)	v	H 1154	Languages	
–Conversation and phrase books (for landscaping industry employees)	v	H 1154	Languages	
–Conversation and phrase books (for lawyers)	v	H 1154	Languages	
–Conversation and phrase books (for library employees)	v	H 1154	Languages	
–Conversation and phrase books (for mathematicians)	v	H 1154	Languages	
–Conversation and phrase books (for medical personnel)	v	H 1154	Languages	
–Conversation and phrase books (for merchants)	v	H 1154	Languages	
–Conversation and phrase books (for meteorologists)	v	H 1154	Languages	
–Conversation and phrase books (for museum employees)	v	H 1154	Languages	
–Conversation and phrase books (for musicians, musicologists, etc.)	v	H 1154	Languages	

SUBDIVISION	SUBFIELD CODE(S)	FREE-FLOATING LIST IN SCM:SH	CATEGORY	USAGE GUIDELINES IN SCM:SH
–Conversation and phrase books (for nutritionists)	v	H 1154	Languages	
–Conversation and phrase books (for personnel department employees)	v	H 1154	Languages	
–Conversation and phrase books (for petroleum workers)	v	H 1154	Languages	
–Conversation and phrase books (for police)	v	H 1154	Languages	
–Conversation and phrase books (for professionals)	v	H 1154	Languages	
–Conversation and phrase books (for restaurant and hotel personnel)	v	H 1154	Languages	
–Conversation and phrase books (for sailors)	v	H 1154	Languages	
–Conversation and phrase books (for school employees)	v	H 1154	Languages	
–Conversation and phrase books (for secretaries)	v	H 1154	Languages	
–Conversation and phrase books (for social workers)	v	H 1154	Languages	
–Conversation and phrase books (for soldiers, etc.)	v	H 1154	Languages	
–Conversation and phrase books (for tourism industry employees)	v	H 1154	Languages	
–Conversion tables	v	H 1095	see *SCM:SH*	
–Cooling *(May Subd Geog)*	x	H 1095 H 1158 H 1180	see *SCM:SH* Materials Plants & crops	
–Cooperative marketing *(May Subd Geog)*	x	H 1147 H 1180	Animals Plants & crops	
–Coordinate constructions	x	H 1154	Languages	

SUBDIVISION	SUBFIELD CODE(S)	FREE-FLOATING LIST IN SCM:SH	CATEGORY	USAGE GUIDELINES IN SCM:SH
–Copies, Curious	x	H 1188	Sacred works	
–Copying	x	H 1148	Art	
–Coronation	x	H 1110	Indiv pers	
–Correspondence	v	H 1100	Classes pers	H 1480
		H 1103	Ethnic groups	H 1480
		H 1110	Indiv pers	H 1480
		H 1120	Families	H 1480
–Correspondence–Microform catalogs	x–v	H 1110	Indiv pers	
–Corrosion *(May Subd Geog)*	x	H 1095	see *SCM:SH*	
		H 1149	Chemicals	
		H 1158	Materials	
		H 1195	Land vehicles	
–Corrosion fatigue *(May Subd Geog)*	x	H 1158	Materials	
–Corrupt practices	x	H 1105	Corp bodies	
–Corrupt practices *(May Subd Geog)*	x	H 1095	see *SCM:SH*	
		H 1151.5	Types schools	
		H 1153	Industries	
–Cossacks *(May Subd Geog)*	x	H 1200	Wars	
–Cost control	x	H 1095	see *SCM:SH*	
		H 1153	Industries	
		H 1159	Military srvces	
–Cost effectiveness	x	H 1095	see *SCM:SH*	
		H 1153	Industries	
–Cost of operation	x	H 1095	see *SCM:SH*	
		H 1195	Land vehicles	
–Costs	x	H 1095	see *SCM:SH*	
		H 1153	Industries	
–Counseling of *(May Subd Geog)*	x	H 1100	Classes pers	
		H 1103	Ethnic groups	
–Counterfeit money *(May Subd Geog)*	x	H 1200	Wars	

SUBDIVISION	SUBFIELD CODE(S)	FREE-FLOATING LIST IN SCM:SH	CATEGORY	USAGE GUIDELINES IN SCM:SH
–Counting *(May Subd Geog)*	x	H 1147	Animals	
		H 1180	Plants & crops	
–Court and courtiers	x	H 1140	Places	
–Court and courtiers–Clothing	x–x	H 1140	Places	
–Court and courtiers–Food	x–x	H 1140	Places	
–Court and courtiers–Language	x–x	H 1140	Places	
–Cracking *(May Subd Geog)*	x	H 1158	Materials	
–Craniology *(May Subd Geog)*	x	H 1103	Ethnic groups	
–Crash tests *(May Subd Geog)*	x	H 1195	Land vehicles	
–Crashworthiness *(May Subd Geog)*	x	H 1195	Land vehicles	
–Credit ratings	x	H 1153	Industries	
–Creeds	v	H 1185	Religions	
		H 1187	Christian denom	
–Creeds–History and criticism	x–x	H 1187	Christian denom	
–Creep *(May Subd Geog)*	x	H 1149	Chemicals	
		H 1158	Materials	
–Crimes against *(May Subd Geog)*	x	H 1100	Classes pers	
		H 1103	Ethnic groups	
–Criminal provisions	x	H 1154.5	Legal topics	
–Criticism, Form	x	H 1188	Sacred works	
–Criticism, Narrative	x	H 1188	Sacred works	
–Criticism, Redaction	x	H 1188	Sacred works	
–Criticism, Textual	x	H 1110	Indiv pers	
		H 1155.6	Lit works/Auth	
		H 1155.8	Lit works/Title	
		H 1156	Literatures	
		H 1188	Sacred works	
–Criticism and interpretation	x	H 1110	Indiv pers	

SUBDIVISION	SUBFIELD CODE(S)	FREE-FLOATING LIST IN SCM:SH	CATEGORY	USAGE GUIDELINES IN SCM:SH
–Criticism and interpretation–History	x–x	H 1110	Indiv pers	
–Criticism and interpretation–History–16th century	x–x–y	H 1110	Indiv pers	
–Criticism and interpretation–History–17th century	x–x–y	H 1110	Indiv pers	
–Criticism and interpretation–History–18th century	x–x–y	H 1110	Indiv pers	
–Criticism and interpretation–History–19th century	x–x–y	H 1110	Indiv pers	
–Criticism and interpretation–History–20th century	x–x–y	H 1110	Indiv pers	
–Criticism and interpretation–History–21st century	x–x–y	H 1110	Indiv pers	
–Criticism, interpretation, etc. *(May Subd Geog)*	x	H 1188	Sacred works	
–Criticism, interpretation, etc.–History	x–x	H 1188	Sacred works	
–Criticism, interpretation, etc.–History–16th century	x–x–y	H 1188	Sacred works	
–Criticism, interpretation, etc.–History–17th century	x–x–y	H 1188	Sacred works	
–Criticism, interpretation, etc.–History–18th century	x–x–y	H 1188	Sacred works	
–Criticism, interpretation, etc.–History–19th century	x–x–y	H 1188	Sacred works	
–Criticism, interpretation, etc.–History–20th century	x–x–y	H 1188	Sacred works	
–Criticism, interpretation, etc.–History–21st century	x–x–y	H 1188	Sacred works	
–Criticism, interpretation, etc.–History–Early church, ca. 30-600	x–x–y	H 1188	Sacred works	

SUBDIVISION	SUBFIELD CODE(S)	FREE-FLOATING LIST IN SCM:SH	CATEGORY	USAGE GUIDELINES IN SCM:SH
–Criticism, interpretation, etc.–History–Middle Ages, 600-1500	x–x–y	H 1188	Sacred works	
–Criticism, interpretation, etc.–History–Modern period, 1500-	x–x–y	H 1188	Sacred works	
–Criticism, interpretation, etc., Jewish	x	H 1188	Sacred works	
–Cross-cultural studies	v	H 1095	see *SCM:SH*	H 1510
–Cross references	v	H 1188	Sacred works	
–Cross-sectional imaging *(May*	x	H 1164	Organs of body	
–Cruise, [date]	x	H 1159	Military srvces	
–Cryopreservation *(May Subd Geog)*	x	H 1164	Organs of body	
–Cryosurgery *(May Subd Geog)*	x	H 1150 H 1164	Diseases Organs of body	
–Cryotherapy *(May Subd Geog)*	x	H 1150	Diseases	
–Cryptography	x	H 1200	Wars	
–Cult *(May Subd Geog)*	x	H 1095 H 1110	see *SCM:SH* Indiv pers	
–Cultural assimilation *(May Subd Geog)*	x	H 1103	Ethnic groups	
–Cultural control *(May Subd Geog)*	x	H 1147 H 1180	Animals Plants & crops	
–Cultural policy	x	H 1140	Places	
–Cultures and culture media *(May Subd Geog)*	x	H 1164	Organs of body	
–Curing *(May Subd Geog)*	x	H 1158	Materials	
–Curricula	x	H 1151	Indiv schools	
–Curricula *(May Subd Geog)*	x	H 1095 H 1151.5	see *SCM:SH* Types schools	

SUBDIVISION	SUBFIELD CODE(S)	FREE-FLOATING LIST IN SCM:SH	CATEGORY	USAGE GUIDELINES IN SCM:SH
–Curricula–Catalogs	x–v	H 1151	Indiv schools	
		H 1151.5	Types schools	
–Customer services	x	H 1105	Corp bodies	
–Customer services *(May Subd Geog)*	x	H 1095	see *SCM:SH*	
		H 1153	Industries	
–Customizing *(May Subd Geog)*	x	H 1161	Musical instrum	
		H 1195	Land vehicles	
–Customs and practices	x	H 1185	Religions	
		H 1186	Relig orders	
		H 1187	Christian denom	
–Cuttings *(May Subd Geog)*	x	H 1180	Plants & crops	
–Cysts *(May Subd Geog)*	x	H 1164	Organs of body	
–Cytochemistry	x	H 1164	Organs of body	
		H 1180	Plants & crops	
–Cytodiagnosis *(May Subd Geog)*	x	H 1150	Diseases	
–Cytogenetics	x	H 1180	Plants & crops	
		H 1147	Animals	
–Cytology	x	H 1147	Animals	
		H 1164	Organs of body	
		H 1180	Plants & crops	
–Cytopathology	x	H 1150	Diseases	
		H 1164	Organs of body	
–Cytotaxonomy *(May Subd Geog)*	x	H 1180	Plants & crops	
–Czech influences	x	H 1156	Literatures	H 1675
–Dalit authors	x	H 1156	Literatures	
–Data processing	x	H 1095	see *SCM:SH*	
		H 1105	Corp bodies	
–Data tape catalogs	v	H 1095	see *SCM:SH*	
–Databases	v	H 1095	see *SCM:SH*	
–Dating	x	H 1095	see *SCM:SH*	

SUBDIVISION	SUBFIELD CODE(S)	FREE-FLOATING LIST IN SCM:SH	CATEGORY	USAGE GUIDELINES IN SCM:SH
–Death	x	H 1100 H 1103	Classes pers Ethnic groups	
–Death and burial	x	H 1110	Indiv pers	
–Death mask	x	H 1110	Indiv pers	
–Decay	x	H 1149	Chemicals	
–Decentralization *(May Subd Geog)*	x	H 1151.5	Types schools	
–Deception *(May Subd Geog)*	x	H 1200	Wars	
–Decision making	x	H 1095 H 1105	see *SCM:SH* Corp bodies	
–Declension	x	H 1154	Languages	
–Decontamination *(May Subd Geog)*	x	H 1149	Chemicals	
–Decoration *(May Subd Geog)*	x	H 1195	Land vehicles	
–Defects *(May Subd Geog)*	x	H 1095 H 1158 H 1195	see *SCM:SH* Materials Land vehicles	
–Defects–Law and legislation *(May Subd Geog)*	x–x	H 1195	Land vehicles	
–Defects–Reporting *(May Subd Geog)*	x–x	H 1095 H 1158 H 1195	see *SCM:SH* Materials Land vehicles	
–Defense measures *(May Subd Geog)*	x	H 1095 H 1153	see *SCM:SH* Industries	
–Defenses	x	H 1140 H 1149.5	Places Colonies	
–Defenses *(May Subd Geog)*	x	H 1147 H 1180	Animals Plants & crops	
–Defenses–Economic aspects	x–x	H 1140	Places	
–Defenses–Law and legislation	x–x	H 1140	Places	
–Definiteness	x	H 1154	Languages	

SUBDIVISION	SUBFIELD CODE(S)	FREE-FLOATING LIST IN SCM:SH	CATEGORY	USAGE GUIDELINES IN SCM:SH
–Degrees	x	H 1151	Indiv schools	
–Deinstitutionalization *(May Subd Geog)*	x	H 1100	Classes pers	
–Deixis	x	H 1154	Languages	
–Deletion	x	H 1154	Languages	
–Demobilization	x	H 1159	Military srvces	
–Demonstratives	x	H 1154	Languages	
–Denaturation	x	H 1149	Chemicals	
–Density	x	H 1149	Chemicals	
		H 1158	Materials	
–Dental care *(May Subd Geog)*	x	H 1100	Classes pers	
		H 1103	Ethnic groups	
		H 1159	Military srvces	
–Deoxidizing *(May Subd Geog)*	x	H 1158	Materials	
–Departments	x	H 1095	see *SCM:SH*	H 713
		H 1151.5	Types schools	
–Dependency grammar	x	H 1154	Languages	
–Dependency on [place]	x	H 1140	Places	
–Dependency on foreign countries	x	H 1140	Places	
–Deputy speakers	x	H 1155	Legis bodies	
–Deregulation *(May Subd Geog)*	x	H 1153	Industries	
–Derivatives *(May Subd Geog)*	x	H 1149	Chemicals	
–Description and travel	x	H 1140	Places	H 1530
		H 1149.5	Colonies	H 1530
–Desertions *(May Subd Geog)*	x	H 1200	Wars	
–Design	x	H 1095	see *SCM:SH*	H 1532
		H 1149	Chemicals	H 1532

SUBDIVISION	SUBFIELD CODE(S)	FREE-FLOATING LIST IN SCM:SH	CATEGORY	USAGE GUIDELINES IN SCM:SH
–Design and construction	x	H 1095 H 1195	see *SCM:SH* Land vehicles	H 1532 H 1532
–Design and construction–Law and legislation *(May Subd Geog)*	x–x	H 1195	Land vehicles	
–Design and construction–Optical methods	x–x	H 1195	Land vehicles	
–Designs and plans	v	H 1095	see *SCM:SH*	H 1532
–Destruction and pillage *(May Subd Geog)*	x	H 1200	Wars	
–Desulfurization *(May Subd Geog)*	x	H 1158	Materials	
–Detection *(May Subd Geog)*	x	H 1147	Animals	
–Deterioration *(May Subd Geog)*	x	H 1095 H 1158	see *SCM:SH* Materials	
–Determiners	x	H 1154	Languages	
–Development *(May Subd Geog)*	x	H 1147 H 1149 H 1180	Animals Chemicals Plants & crops	
–Development–Endocrine aspects	x–x	H 1147	Animals	
–Devotional literature	v	H 1188	Sacred works	
–Devotional use	x	H 1188	Sacred works	
–Dewatering *(May Subd Geog)*	x	H 1158	Materials	
–Diacritics	x	H 1154	Languages	
–Diagnosis *(May Subd Geog)*	x	H 1150	Diseases	
–Diagnostic use *(May Subd Geog)*	x	H 1149	Chemicals	
–Dialectology	x	H 1154	Languages	
–Dialects *(May Subd Geog)*	x	H 1154	Languages	
–Dialects–Conversation and phrase books	x–v	H 1154	Languages	

SUBDIVISION	SUBFIELD CODE(S)	FREE-FLOATING LIST IN SCM:SH	CATEGORY	USAGE GUIDELINES IN SCM:SH	
–Dialects–Glossaries, vocabularies, etc.	x–v	H 1154	Languages		
–Dialects–Grammar	x–x	H 1154	Languages		
–Dialects–Lexicology	x–x	H 1154	Languages		
–Dialects–Morphology	x–x	H 1154	Languages		
–Dialects–Phonetics	x–x	H 1154	Languages		
–Dialects–Phonology	x–x	H 1154	Languages		
–Dialects–Research *(May Subd Geog)*	x–x	H 1154	Languages		
–Dialects–Research–Law and legislation *(May Subd Geog)*	x–x–x	H 1154	Languages		
–Dialects–Syntax	x–x	H 1154	Languages		
–Dialects–Texts	x–v	H 1154	Languages		
–Diaries	v	H 1100	Classes pers	H 1538	
		H 1103	Ethnic groups	H 1538	
		H 1110	Indiv pers	H 1538	
		H 1120	Families	H 1538	
		H 1159	Military srvces	H 1538	
–Diction	x	H 1154	Languages		
–Dictionaries	v	H 1095	see *SCM:SH*	H 1540	
		H 1154	Languages	H 1540	
–Dictionaries–Early works to 1700	v–v	H 1154	Languages		
–Dictionaries–French, [Italian, etc.]	v–x	H 1095	see *SCM:SH*	H 1540	
		H 1154	Languages	H 1540	
–Dictionaries–Polyglot	v–x	H 1095	see *SCM:SH*	H 1540	
		H 1154	Languages	H 1540	
–Dictionaries, Juvenile	v	H 1095	see *SCM:SH*	H 1540	H 1690
		H 1154	Languages	H 1540	H 1690
–Dictionaries, Juvenile–Hebrew, [Italian, etc.]	v–x	H 1154	Languages	H 1540	H 1690

SUBDIVISION	SUBFIELD CODE(S)	FREE-FLOATING LIST IN SCM:SH	CATEGORY	USAGE GUIDELINES IN SCM:SH
–Diet therapy *(May Subd Geog)*	x	H 1150	Diseases	
–Diet therapy–Recipes	x–v	H 1150	Diseases	
–Differentials	x	H 1195	Land vehicles	
–Differentiation	x	H 1164	Organs of body	
–Differentiation therapy *(May Subd Geog)*	x	H 1150	Diseases	
–Diffusion rate	x	H 1149	Chemicals	
–Digestive organs	x	H 1147	Animals	
–Digests	v	H 1154.5	Legal topics	H 1550
–Digitization *(May Subd Geog)*	x	H 1095	see *SCM:SH*	
–Dilatation *(May Subd Geog)*	x	H 1164	Organs of body	
–Diminutives	x	H 1154	Languages	
–Dioceses *(May Subd Geog)*	x	H 1187	Christian denom	
–Diphthongs	x	H 1154	Languages	
–Diplomatic history	x	H 1200	Wars	
–Diplomatic service	x	H 1187	Christian denom	
–Dipole moments	x	H 1149	Chemicals	
–Direct object	x	H 1154	Languages	
–Directories	v	H 1095	see *SCM:SH*	H 1558
		H 1100	Classes pers	H 1558
		H 1103	Ethnic groups	H 1558
		H 1105	Corp bodies	H 1558
		H 1120	Families	H 1558
		H 1140	Places	H 1558
–Disc brakes	x	H 1195	Land vehicles	
–Disciples	x	H 1110	Indiv pers	

SUBDIVISION	SUBFIELD CODE(S)	FREE-FLOATING LIST IN SCM:SH	CATEGORY	USAGE GUIDELINES IN SCM:SH
–Discipline	x	H 1095	see *SCM:SH*	
		H 1100	Classes pers	
		H 1105	Corp bodies	
		H 1185	Religions	
		H 1187	Christian denom	
–Discography	v	H 1095	see *SCM:SH*	H 1361
		H 1100	Classes pers	H 1361
		H 1103	Ethnic groups	H 1361
		H 1105	Corp bodies	H 1361
		H 1110	Indiv pers	H 1361
		H 1160	Musical comps	H 1361
–Discography–Methodology	x–x	H 1160	Musical comps	
–Discourse analysis	x	H 1154	Languages	
–Discovery and exploration	x	H 1140	Places	H 1564
		H 1149.5	Colonies	H 1564
–Discovery and exploration–French, [Spanish, etc.]	x–x	H 1140	Places	H 1564
–Disease and pest resistance *(May Subd Geog)*	x	H 1180	Plants & crops	
–Disease and pest resistance–Genetic aspects	x–x	H 1180	Plants & crops	
–Disease-free stock *(May Subd Geog)*	x	H 1180	Plants & crops	
–Diseases *(May Subd Geog)*	x	H 1100	Classes pers	
		H 1103	Ethnic groups	
		H 1147	Animals	
		H 1164	Organs of body	
–Diseases–Alternative treatment *(May Subd Geog)*	x–x	H 1147	Animals	
–Diseases–Chemotherapy *(May Subd Geog)*	x–x	H 1147	Animals	
–Diseases–Chiropractic treatment *(May Subd Geog)*	x–x	H 1147	Animals	
–Diseases–Diagnosis *(May Subd Geog)*	x–x	H 1147	Animals	

SUBDIVISION	SUBFIELD CODE(S)	FREE-FLOATING LIST IN SCM:SH	CATEGORY	USAGE GUIDELINES IN SCM:SH
–Diseases–Diet therapy *(May Subd Geog)*	x–x	H 1147	Animals	
–Diseases–Epidemiology	x–x	H 1147	Animals	
–Diseases–Genetic aspects	x–x	H 1147	Animals	
–Diseases–Homeopathic treatment *(May Subd Geog)*	x–x	H 1147	Animals	
–Diseases–Molecular aspects	x–x	H 1147	Animals	
–Diseases–Nursing *(May Subd Geog)*	x–x	H 1147	Animals	
–Diseases–Nutritional aspects *(May Subd Geog)*	x–x	H 1147	Animals	
–Diseases–Prevention	x–x	H 1147	Animals	
–Diseases–Treatment *(May Subd Geog)*	x–x	H 1147	Animals	
–Diseases and pests *(May Subd Geog)*	x	H 1180	Plants & crops	
–Diseases and pests–Biological control *(May Subd Geog)*	x–x	H 1180	Plants & crops	
–Diseases and pests–Control *(May Subd Geog)*	x–x	H 1180	Plants & crops	
–Diseases and pests–Control– Environmental aspects *(May Subd Geog)*	x–x–x	H 1180	Plants & crops	
–Diseases and pests–Cultural control *(May Subd Geog)*	x–x	H 1180	Plants & crops	
–Diseases and pests–Identification	x–v	H 1180	Plants & crops	
–Diseases and pests–Integrated control *(May Subd Geog)*	x–x	H 1180	Plants & crops	
–Diseases and pests–Monitoring *(May Subd Geog)*	x–x	H 1180	Plants & crops	
–Diseases and pests–Nutritional aspects *(May Subd Geog)*	x–x	H 1180	Plants & crops	

SUBDIVISION	SUBFIELD CODE(S)	FREE-FLOATING LIST IN SCM:SH	CATEGORY	USAGE GUIDELINES IN SCM:SH
–Dislocation *(May Subd Geog)*	x	H 1164	Organs of body	
–Dismissal of *(May Subd Geog)*	x	H 1100	Classes pers	
–Dispersal *(May Subd Geog)*	x	H 1147 H 1180	Animals Plants & crops	
–Displacement	x	H 1164	Organs of body	
–Dissection *(May Subd Geog)*	x	H 1147 H 1164	Animals Organs of body	
–Dissertations	x	H 1151	Indiv schools	H 1570
–Dissertations–Style manuals	x–v	H 1151	Indiv schools	
–Dissimilation	x	H 1154	Languages	
–Dissolution	x	H 1155 H 1158	Legis bodies Materials	
–Distances, etc.	x	H 1140	Places	
–Divorce	x	H 1110	Indiv pers	
–Doctrines	x	H 1185 H 1187	Religions Christian denom	
–Doctrines–History	x–x	H 1187	Christian denom	
–Doctrines–History–Modern period, 1500-	x–x–y	H 1187	Christian denom	
–Documentation *(May Subd Geog)*	x	H 1095	see *SCM:SH*	
–Domestic animals *(May Subd Geog)*	x	H 1103	Ethnic groups	
–Doors	x	H 1195	Land vehicles	
–Dormancy *(May Subd Geog)*	x	H 1147 H 1180	Animals Plants & crops	
–Dose-response relationship	x	H 1149	Chemicals	
–Dosimetric treatment *(May Subd Geog)*	x	H 1150	Diseases	
–Draft resisters *(May Subd Geog)*	x	H 1200	Wars	

SUBDIVISION	SUBFIELD CODE(S)	FREE-FLOATING LIST IN SCM:SH	CATEGORY	USAGE GUIDELINES IN SCM:SH
–Drama	v	H 1095	see *SCM:SH*	H 1780
		H 1100	Classes pers	H 1780
		H 1103	Ethnic groups	H 1780
		H 1105	Corp bodies	H 1780
		H 1110	Indiv pers	H 1780
		H 1120	Families	H 1780
		H 1140	Places	H 1780
–Dramatic production	x	H 1110	Indiv pers	
		H 1155.8	Lit works/Title	
–Dramatic works	x	H 1110	Indiv pers	
–Dramaturgy	x	H 1110	Indiv pers	
–Dravidian authors	x	H 1156	Literatures	
–Drawings	v	H 1095	see *SCM:SH*	
–Drill and tactics	x	H 1159	Military srvces	
–Drill and tactics–Handbooks, manuals, etc.	x–v	H 1159	Military srvces	
–Drought tolerance *(May Subd Geog)*	x	H 1180	Plants & crops	
–Drug testing *(May Subd Geog)*	x	H 1100	Classes pers	
–Drug use	x	H 1110	Indiv pers	
–Drug use *(May Subd Geog)*	x	H 1100	Classes pers	
		H 1103	Ethnic groups	
–Druze authors	x	H 1156	Literatures	
–Drying *(May Subd Geog)*	x	H 1095	see *SCM:SH*	
		H 1158	Materials	
		H 1180	Plants & crops	
–Ductility	x	H 1158	Materials	
–Dust control *(May Subd Geog)*	x	H 1095	see *SCM:SH*	
		H 1153	Industries	
–Dwellings *(May Subd Geog)*	x	H 1100	Classes pers	
		H 1103	Ethnic groups	
–Dynamics	x	H 1195	Land vehicles	

SUBDIVISION	SUBFIELD CODE(S)	FREE-FLOATING LIST IN SCM:SH	CATEGORY	USAGE GUIDELINES IN SCM:SH
–Early modern, 1500-1700	y	H 1154	Languages	
		H 1155.2	Groups lit auth	
		H 1156	Literatures	
–Early modern and Elizabethan, 1500-1600	y	H 1156	Drama	
–Early works to 1800	v	H 1095	see *SCM:SH*	H 1576
		H 1100	Classes pers	H 1576
		H 1103	Ethnic groups	H 1576
		H 1140	Places	H 1576
–Earthquake effects *(May Subd Geog)*	x	H 1095	see *SCM:SH*	
–Eclectic treatment *(May Subd Geog)*	x	H 1150	Diseases	
–Ecology *(May Subd Geog)*	x	H 1147	Animals	
		H 1180	Plants & crops	
–Econometric models	x	H 1095	see *SCM:SH*	H 2040
		H 1153	Industries	H 2040
–Economic aspects *(May Subd Geog)*	x	H 1095	see *SCM:SH*	
		H 1200	Wars	
–Economic conditions	x	H 1100	Classes pers	H 1578
		H 1103	Ethnic groups	H 1578
		H 1140	Places	H 1578
		H 1149.5	Colonies	H 1578
–Economic conditions–16th century	x–y	H 1100	Classes pers	H 1578
		H 1103	Ethnic groups	H 1578
		H 1140	Places	H 1578
–Economic conditions–17th century	x–y	H 1100	Classes pers	H 1578
		H 1103	Ethnic groups	H 1578
		H 1140	Places	H 1578
–Economic conditions–18th century	x–y	H 1100	Classes pers	H 1578
		H 1103	Ethnic groups	H 1578
		H 1140	Places	H 1578
–Economic conditions–19th century	x–y	H 1100	Classes pers	H 1578
		H 1103	Ethnic groups	H 1578
		H 1140	Places	H 1578

SUBDIVISION	SUBFIELD CODE(S)	FREE-FLOATING LIST IN SCM:SH	CATEGORY	USAGE GUIDELINES IN SCM:SH	
–Economic conditions–20th century	x–y	H 1100	Classes pers	H 1578	
		H 1103	Ethnic groups	H 1578	
		H 1140	Places	H 1578	
–Economic conditions–21st century	x–y	H 1100	Classes pers	H 1578	
		H 1103	Ethnic groups	H 1578	
		H 1140	Places	H 1578	
–Economic conditions–[period subdivision]–Regional disparities	x–y–x	H 1140	Places		
–Economic conditions–Regional disparities	x–x	H 1140	Places		
–Economic integration	x	H 1140	Places		
–Economic policy	x	H 1140	Places		
		H 1149.5	Colonies		
–Ecophysiology *(May Subd Geog)*	x	H 1147	Animals		
		H 1180	Plants & crops		
–Editions, Curious	x	H 1188	Sacred works		
–Edo period, 1600-1868	y	H 1148	Japanese art		
–Education *(May Subd Geog)*	x	H 1100	Classes pers	H 1579	H 2217
		H 1103	Ethnic groups	H 1579	
		H 1186	Relig orders	H 1579	
		H 1187	Christian denom	H 1579	
–Education–Law and legislation *(May Subd Geog)*	x–x	H 1103	Ethnic groups		
–Education (Continuing education) *(May Subd Geog)*	x	H 1100	Classes pers	H 1579	
		H 1103	Ethnic groups	H 1579	
–Education (Early childhood) *(May Subd Geog)*	x	H 1100	Classes pers	H 1579	
		H 1103	Ethnic groups	H 1579	
–Education (Elementary) *(May Subd Geog)*	x	H 1100	Classes pers	H 1579	
		H 1103	Ethnic groups	H 1579	
–Education (Graduate) *(May Subd Geog)*	x	H 1100	Classes pers	H 1579	
		H 1103	Ethnic groups	H 1579	

SUBDIVISION	SUBFIELD CODE(S)	FREE-FLOATING LIST IN SCM:SH	CATEGORY	USAGE GUIDELINES IN SCM:SH
–Education (Higher) (May Subd Geog)	x	H 1100 H 1103	Classes pers Ethnic groups	H 1579 H 1579
–Education (Middle school) (May Subd Geog)	x	H 1100 H 1103	Classes pers Ethnic groups	H 1579 H 1579
–Education (Preschool) (May Subd Geog)	x	H 1100 H 1103	Classes pers Ethnic groups	H 1579 H 1579
–Education (Primary) (May Subd Geog)	x	H 1100 H 1103	Classes pers Ethnic groups	H 1579 H 1579
–Education (Secondary) (May Subd Geog)	x	H 1100 H 1103	Classes pers Ethnic groups	H 1579 H 1579
–Education and the war, [revolution, etc.]	x	H 1200	Wars	
–Effect of acid deposition on (May Subd Geog)	x	H 1180	Plants & crops	H 1580
–Effect of acid precipitation on (May Subd Geog)	x	H 1147 H 1180	Animals Plants & crops	H 1580 H 1580
–Effect of air pollution on (May Subd Geog)	x	H 1180	Plants & crops	H 1580
–Effect of air pollution on– Genetic aspects	x	H 1180	Plants & crops	
–Effect of aircraft on (May Subd Geog)	x	H 1147	Animals	H 1580
–Effect of altitude on (May Subd Geog)	x	H 1147	Animals	H 1580
–Effect of aluminum sulfate on (May Subd Geog)	x	H 1180	Plants & crops	H 1580
–Effect of arsenic on (May Subd Geog)	x	H 1180	Plants & crops	H 1580
–Effect of atmospheric carbon dioxide on (May Subd Geog)	x	H 1180	Plants & crops	H 1580
–Effect of atmospheric deposition on (May Subd Geog)	x	H 1180	Plants & crops	H 1580

SUBDIVISION	SUBFIELD CODE(S)	FREE-FLOATING LIST IN SCM:SH	CATEGORY	USAGE GUIDELINES IN SCM:SH
–Effect of atmospheric nitrogen dioxide on *(May Subd Geog)*	x	H 1180	Plants & crops	H 1580
–Effect of atmospheric ozone on *(May Subd Geog)*	x	H 1180	Plants & crops	H 1580
–Effect of automation on *(May Subd Geog)*	x	H 1100	Classes pers	H 1580
–Effect of browsing on *(May Subd Geog)*	x	H 1180	Plants & crops	H 1580
–Effect of cadmium on *(May Subd Geog)*	x	H 1180	Plants & crops	H 1580
–Effect of chemicals on *(May Subd Geog)*	x	H 1147 H 1164	Animals Organs of body	H 1580 H 1580
–Effect of cold on *(May Subd Geog)*	x	H 1147 H 1164 H 1180	Animals Organs of body Plants & crops	H 1580 H 1580 H 1580
–Effect of contaminated sediments on *(May Subd Geog)*	x	H 1147	Animals	H 1580
–Effect of dams on *(May Subd Geog)*	x	H 1147	Animals	H 1580
–Effect of dichlorophenoxyacetic acid on *(May Subd Geog)*	x	H 1180	Plants & crops	H 1580
–Effect of dredging on *(May Subd Subd Geog)*	x	H 1147 H 1180	Animals Plants & crops	H 1580 H 1580
–Effect of drought on *(May Subd Geog)*	x	H 1147 H 1180	Animals Plants & crops	H 1580 H 1580
–Effect of drugs on *(May Subd Geog)*	x	H 1147 H 1164	Animals Organs of body	H 1580 H 1580
–Effect of environment on *(May Subd Geog)*	x	H 1195	Land vehicles	H 1580
–Effect of ethephon on *(May Subd Geog)*	x	H 1180	Plants & crops	H 1580
–Effect of exotic animals on *(May Subd Geog)*	x	H 1147	Animals	H 1580

SUBDIVISION	SUBFIELD CODE(S)	FREE-FLOATING LIST IN SCM:SH	CATEGORY	USAGE GUIDELINES IN SCM:SH
–Effect of explosive devices on *(May Subd Geog)*	x	H 1195	Land vehicles	H 1580
–Effect of factory and trade waste on *(May Subd Geog)*	x	H 1180	Plants & crops	H 1580
–Effect of ferrous sulfate on *(May Subd Geog)*	x	H 1180	Plants & crops	H 1580
–Effect of fires on *(May Subd Geog)*	x	H 1147 H 1180	Animals Plants & crops	H 1580 H 1580
–Effect of fires on–Genetic aspects	x–x	H 1180	Plants & crops	
–Effect of fishing on *(May Subd Geog)*	x	H 1147	Animals	H 1580
–Effect of floods on *(May Subd Geog)*	x	H 1147 H 1180	Animals Plants & crops	H 1580 H 1580
–Effect of fluorides on *(May Subd Geog)*	x	H 1180	Plants & crops	H 1580
–Effect of fluorine on *(May Subd Geog)*	x	H 1180	Plants & crops	H 1580
–Effect of forest management on *(May Subd Geog)*	x	H 1147	Animals	H 1580
–Effect of freezes on *(May Subd Geog)*	x	H 1180	Plants & crops	H 1580
–Effect of gamma rays on *(May Subd Geog)*	x	H 1180	Plants & crops	H 1580
–Effect of gases on *(May Subd Geog)*	x	H 1180	Plants & crops	H 1580
–Effect of global warming on *(May Subd Geog)*	x	H 1180	Plants & crops	H 1580
–Effect of glyphosate on *(May Subd Geog)*	x	H 1180	Plants & crops	H 1580
–Effect of grazing on *(May Subd Geog)*	x	H 1180	Plants & crops	H 1580

SUBDIVISION	SUBFIELD CODE(S)	FREE-FLOATING LIST IN SCM:SH	CATEGORY	USAGE GUIDELINES IN SCM:SH
–Effect of greenhouse gases on *(May Subd Geog)*	x	H 1180	Plants & crops	H 1580
–Effect of habitat modification on *(May Subd Geog)*	x	H 1147	Animals	H 1580
–Effect of heat on *(May Subd Geog)*	x	H 1164	Organs of body	H 1580
–Effect of heavy metals on *(May Subd Geog)*	x	H 1147 H 1180	Animals Plants & crops	H 1580 H 1580
–Effect of high temperatures on *(May Subd Geog)*	x	H 1158	Materials	H 1580
–Effect of human beings on *(May Subd Geog)*	x	H 1147	Animals	H 1580
–Effect of hunting on *(May Subd Geog)*	x	H 1147	Animals	H 1580
–Effect of ice on *(May Subd Geog)*	x	H 1180	Plants & crops	H 1580
–Effect of implants on *(May Subd Geog)*	x	H 1164	Organs of body	H 1580
–Effect of imprisonment on *(May Subd Geog)*	x	H 1100	Classes pers	H 1580
–Effect of insecticides on *(May Subd Geog)*	x	H 1147	Animals	H 1580
–Effect of iron on *(May Subd Geog)*	x	H 1180	Plants & crops	H 1580
–Effect of lasers on *(May Subd Geog)*	x	H 1158	Materials	H 1580
–Effect of light on *(May Subd Geog)*	x	H 1147 H 1180	Animals Plants & crops	H 1580 H 1580
–Effect of logging on *(May Subd Geog)*	x	H 1147	Animals	H 1580
–Effect of low temperatures on *(May Subd Geog)*	x	H 1158	Materials	H 1580
–Effect of magnesium on *(May Subd Geog)*	x	H 1180	Plants & crops	H 1580

SUBDIVISION	SUBFIELD CODE(S)	FREE-FLOATING LIST IN SCM:SH	CATEGORY	USAGE GUIDELINES IN SCM:SH
–Effect of manganese on *(May Subd Geog)*	x	H 1180	Plants & crops	H 1580
–Effect of metals on *(May Subd Geog)*	x	H 1147 H 1164	Animals Organs of body	H 1580 H 1580
–Effect of minerals on *(May Subd Geog)*	x	H 1180	Plants & crops	H 1580
–Effect of music on *(May Subd Geog)*	x	H 1147	Animals	H 1580
–Effect of noise on *(May Subd Geog)*	x	H 1147	Animals	H 1580
–Effect of odors on *(May Subd Geog)*	x	H 1147	Animals	H 1580
–Effect of off-road vehicles on *(May Subd Geog)*	x	H 1180	Plants & crops	H 1580
–Effect of oil spills on *(May Subd Geog)*	x	H 1147	Animals	H 1580
–Effect of oxygen on *(May Subd Geog)*	x	H 1180	Plants & crops	H 1580
–Effect of ozone on *(May Subd Geog)*	x	H 1180	Plants & crops	H 1580
–Effect of pesticides on *(May Subd Geog)*	x	H 1147 H 1180	Animals Plants & crops	H 1580 H 1580
–Effect of pollution on *(May Subd Geog)*	x	H 1147 H 1180	Animals Plants & crops	H 1580 H 1580
–Effect of potassium on *(May Subd Geog)*	x	H 1180	Plants & crops	H 1580
–Effect of predation on *(May Subd Geog)*	x	H 1147	Animals	H 1580
–Effect of radiation on *(May Subd Geog)*	x	H 1147 H 1149 H 1158 H 1164 H 1180	Animals Chemicals Materials Organs of body Plants & crops	H 1580 H 1580 H 1580 H 1580 H 1580
–Effect of radioactive pollution on *(May Subd Geog)*	x	H 1147 H 1180	Animals Plants & crops	H 1580 H 1580

SUBDIVISION	SUBFIELD CODE(S)	FREE-FLOATING LIST IN SCM:SH	CATEGORY	USAGE GUIDELINES IN SCM:SH
–Effect of roads on *(May Subd Geog)*	x	H 1147	Animals	H 1580
–Effect of salt on *(May Subd Geog)*	x	H 1147	Animals	H 1580
		H 1158	Materials	H 1580
		H 1180	Plants & crops	H 1580
–Effect of sediments on *(May Subd Geog)*	x	H 1147	Animals	H 1580
–Effect of soil acidity on *(May Subd Geog)*	x	H 1180	Plants & crops	H 1580
–Effect of sound on *(May Subd Geog)*	x	H 1147	Animals	H 1580
–Effect of space flight on	x	H 1164	Organs of body	H 1580
–Effect of storms on *(May Subd Geog)*	x	H 1147	Animals	H 1580
–Effect of stray currents on *(May Subd Geog)*	x	H 1147	Animals	H 1580
–Effect of stress on *(May Subd Geog)*	x	H 1147	Animals	H 1580
		H 1164	Organs of body	H 1580
		H 1180	Plants & crops	H 1580
–Effect of sulfates on *(May Subd Geog)*	x	H 1180	Plants & crops	H 1580
–Effect of sulfur on *(May Subd Geog)*	x	H 1180	Plants & crops	H 1580
–Effect of surface active agents on *(May Subd Geog)*	x	H 1147	Animals	H 1580
–Effect of technological innovations on *(May Subd Geog)*	x	H 1100	Classes pers	H 1580
–Effect of temperature on *(May Subd Geog)*	x	H 1147	Animals	H 1580
		H 1158	Materials	H 1580
		H 1180	Plants & crops	H 1580
–Effect of thermal pollution on *(May Subd Geog)*	x	H 1180	Plants & crops	H 1580

SUBDIVISION	SUBFIELD CODE(S)	FREE-FLOATING LIST IN SCM:SH	CATEGORY	USAGE GUIDELINES IN SCM:SH
–Effect of trampling on *(May Subd Geog)*	x	H 1180	Plants & crops	H 1580
–Effect of tricholoroethylene on *(May Subd Geog)*	x	H 1180	Plants & crops	H 1580
–Effect of turbidity on *(May Subd Geog)*	x	H 1147 H 1180	Animals Plants & crops	H 1580 H 1580
–Effect of ultraviolet radiation on *(May Subd Geog)*	x	H 1147 H 1180	Animals Plants & crops	H 1580 H 1580
–Effect of vibration on *(May Subd Geog)*	x	H 1164	Organs of body	H 1580
–Effect of volcanic eruptions on *(May Subd Geog)*	x	H 1147 H 1180	Animals Plants & crops	H 1580 H 1580
–Effect of water acidification on *(May Subd Geog)*	x	H 1147	Animals	H 1580
–Effect of water currents on *(May Subd Geog)*	x	H 1147	Animals	H 1580
–Effect of water levels on *(May Subd Geog)*	x	H 1147 H 1180	Animals Plants & crops	H 1580 H 1580
–Effect of water pollution on *(May Subd Geog)*	x	H 1147 H 1180	Animals Plants & crops	H 1580
–Effect of water quality on *(May Subd Geog)*	x	H 1147	Animals	H 1580
–Effect of water waves on *(May Subd Geog)*	x	H 1180	Plants & crops	H 1580
–Effect of wind on *(May Subd Geog)*	x	H 1180	Plants & crops	H 1580
–Effectiveness *(May Subd Geog)*	x	H 1149	Chemicals	
–Eggs *(May Subd Geog)*	x	H 1147	Animals	
–Eggs–Counting *(May Subd Geog)*	x–x	H 1147	Animals	
–Eggs–Dispersal *(May Subd Geog)*	x–x	H 1147	Animals	
–Eggs–Geographical distribution	x–x	H 1147	Animals	

SUBDIVISION	SUBFIELD CODE(S)	FREE-FLOATING LIST IN SCM:SH	CATEGORY	USAGE GUIDELINES IN SCM:SH
–Eggs–Incubation *(May Subd Geog)*	x–x	H 1147	Animals	
–Egyptian influences	x	H 1156	Literatures	H 1675
–Elastic properties *(May Subd Geog)*	x	H 1158	Materials	
–Election districts	x	H 1155	Legis bodies	
–Elections	x	H 1105 H 1155	Corp bodies Legis bodies	
–Elections, [date]	x	H 1155	Legis bodies	
–Elective system	x	H 1151.5	Types schools	
–Electric equipment *(May Subd Geog)*	x	H 1153 H 1195	Industries Land vehicles	
–Electric generators *(May Subd Geog)*	x	H 1195	Land vehicles	
–Electric installations	x	H 1159	Military srvces	
–Electric properties *(May Subd Geog)*	x	H 1149 H 1158 H 1164 H 1180	Chemicals Materials Organs of body Plants & crops	
–Electric wiring	x	H 1195	Land vehicles	
–Electromechanical analogies	x	H 1095	see *SCM:SH*	H 2040
–Electrometallurgy	x	H 1149	Chemicals	
–Electronic discussion groups	v	H 1095	see *SCM:SH*	
–Electronic equipment *(May Subd Geog)*	x	H 1153 H 1195	Industries Land vehicles	
–Electronic information resources	x	H 1095	see *SCM:SH*	
–Electronic installations	x	H 1159	Military srvces	
–Electronic intelligence *(May Subd Geog)*	x	H 1200	Wars	
–Electronic publishing	x	H 1095	see *SCM:SH*	

SUBDIVISION	SUBFIELD CODE(S)	FREE-FLOATING LIST IN SCM:SH	CATEGORY	USAGE GUIDELINES IN SCM:SH
–Electronic technicians	x	H 1159	Military srvces	
–Elision	x	H 1154	Languages	
–Ellipsis	x	H 1154	Languages	
–Embouchure	x	H 1161	Musical instum	
–Embrittlement	x	H 1158	Materials	
–Embryology	x	H 1147 H 1180	Animals Plants & crops	
–Embryos *(May Subd Geog)*	x	H 1147 H 1180	Animals Plants & crops	
–Embryos–Anatomy	x–x	H 1147	Animals	
–Embryos–Effect of ultraviolet radiation on *(May Subd Geog)*	x–x	H 1147	Animals	H 1580
–Embryos–Nutrition *(May Subd Geog)*	x–x	H 1180	Plants & crops	
–Embryos–Physiology *(May Subd Geog)*	x–x	H 1147	Animals	
–Embryos–Transplantation *(May Subd Geog)*	x–x	H 1147	Animals	
–Emigration and immigration	x	H 1140 H 1149.5	Places Colonies	H 1581 H 1581
–Emigration and immigration–Economic aspects	x–x	H 1140	Places	H 1581
–Emigration and immigration–Government policy	x–x	H 1140	Places	H 1581
–Emigration and immigration–Religious aspects	x–x	H 1140	Places	H 1581
–Emigration and immigration–Religious aspects–Baptists, [Catholic Church, etc.]	x–x–x	H 1140	Places	H 1581

SUBDIVISION	SUBFIELD CODE(S)	FREE-FLOATING LIST IN SCM:SH	CATEGORY	USAGE GUIDELINES IN SCM:SH
–Emigration and immigration–Religious aspects–Buddhism, [Christianity, etc.]	x–x–x	H 1140	Places	H 1581
–Emigration and immigration–Social aspects	x–x	H 1140	Places	H 1581
–Emphasis	x	H 1154	Languages	
–Employees	x	H 1095	see *SCM:SH*	
		H 1105	Corp bodies	
		H 1110	Indiv pers	
		H 1151	Indiv schools	
		H 1151.5	Types schools	
		H 1153	Industries	
		H 1187	Christian denom	
–Employees–Diseases *(May Subd Geog)*	x–x	H 1153	Industries	
–Employees–Effect of technological innovations on *(May Subd Geog)*	x–x	H 1153	Industries	
–Employees–Health and hygiene *(May Subd Geog)*	x–x	H 1153	Industries	
–Employees–Job descriptions *(May Subd Geog)*	x–v	H 1153	Industries	
–Employees–Legal status, laws, etc. *(May Subd Geog)*	x–x	H 1153	Industries	
–Employees–Medical care *(May Subd Geog)*	x–x	H 1153	Industries	
–Employees–Pensions *(May Subd Geog)*	x–x	H 1153	Industries	
–Employees–Pensions–Law and legislation *(May Subd Geog)*	x–x–x	H 1153	Industries	
–Employees–Supply and demand *(May Subd Geog)*	x–x	H 1153	Industries	
–Employees–Training of *(May Subd Geog)*	x–x	H 1153	Industries	

SUBDIVISION	SUBFIELD CODE(S)	FREE-FLOATING LIST IN SCM:SH	CATEGORY	USAGE GUIDELINES IN SCM:SH
–Employment *(May Subd Geog)*	x	H 1100 H 1103	Classes pers Ethnic groups	
–Employment–Foreign countries	x–z	H 1100 H 1103	Classes pers Ethnic groups	
–Enclitics	x	H 1154	Languages	
–Encyclopedias	v	H 1095	see *SCM:SH*	
–Encyclopedias, Juvenile	v	H 1095	see *SCM:SH*	
–Endocrine aspects	x	H 1150	Diseases	
–Endocrinology	x	H 1147	Animals	
–Endoscopic surgery *(May Subd Geog)*	x	H 1150 H 1164	Diseases Organs of body	
–Endoscopic surgery–Complications *(May Subd Geog)*	x–x	H 1164	Organs of body	
–Endowments	x	H 1095 H 1105	see *SCM:SH* Corp bodies	
–Energy conservation *(May Subd Geog)*	x	H 1095 H 1153	see *SCM:SH* Industries	
–Energy consumption	x	H 1159	Military srvces	
–Energy consumption *(May Subd Geog)*	x	H 1095 H 1153	see *SCM:SH* Industries	
–Engineering and construction	x	H 1200	Wars	
–English influences	x	H 1156	Literatures	H 1675
–Entrance examinations	x	H 1151 H 1151.5	Indiv schools Types schools	
–Entrance examinations–Law and legislation *(May Subd Geog)*	x–x	H 1151.5	Types schools	
–Entrance examinations–Study guides	x–v	H 1151.5	Types schools	
–Entrance requirements	x	H 1151 H 1151.5	Indiv schools Types schools	

SUBDIVISION	SUBFIELD CODE(S)	FREE-FLOATING LIST IN SCM:SH	CATEGORY	USAGE GUIDELINES IN SCM:SH
–Entrance requirements–[subject]	x	H 1151	Indiv schools	
–Environmental aspects	x	H 1159	Military srvces	
–Environmental aspects (May Subd Geog)	x	H 1095 H 1149 H 1150 H 1153 H 1158 H 1195 H 1200	see SCM:SH Chemicals Diseases Industries Materials Land vehicles Wars	
–Environmental conditions	x	H 1140	Places	
–Environmental enrichment (May Subd Geog)	x	H 1147	Animals	
–Environmental testing (May Subd Geog)	x	H 1158	Materials	
–Epidemiology	x	H 1150	Diseases	
–Epithets	x	H 1154	Languages	
–Eponyms	x	H 1154	Languages	
–Equipment	x	H 1159	Military srvces	
–Equipment–Quality control	x–x	H 1159	Military srvces	
–Equipment and supplies	x	H 1095 H 1105 H 1147 H 1153 H 1180 H 1195 H 1200	see SCM:SH Corp bodies Animals Industries Plants & crops Land vehicles Wars	
–Ergative constructions	x	H 1154	Languages	
–Erosion (May Subd Geog)	x	H 1158	Materials	
–Errors of usage	x	H 1154	Languages	
–Eruption, [date]	x	H 1140	Places	
–Eruptions	x	H 1140	Places	

SUBDIVISION	SUBFIELD CODE(S)	FREE-FLOATING LIST IN SCM:SH	CATEGORY	USAGE GUIDELINES IN SCM:SH
–Essence, genius, nature	x	H 1185	Religions	
–Estate	x	H 1110	Indiv pers	
–Estimates *(May Subd Geog)*	x	H 1095 H 1153	see *SCM:SH* Industries	
–Etching *(May Subd Geog)*	x	H 1158	Materials	
–Ethics	x	H 1110 H 1155	Indiv pers Legis bodies	
–Ethnic identity	x	H 1103	Ethnic groups	
–Ethnic relations	x	H 1140	Places	
–Ethnic relations–Economic aspects	x–x	H 1140	Places	
–Ethnic relations–Political aspects	x–x	H 1140	Places	
–Ethnobiology *(May Subd Geog)*	x	H 1103	Ethnic groups	
–Ethnobotany *(May Subd Geog)*	x	H 1103	Ethnic groups	
–Ethnological collections	x	H 1105 H 1110 H 1120	Corp bodies Indiv pers Families	H 1427 H 1427 H 1427
–Ethnomusicological collections	x	H 1105 H 1110 H 1120	Corp bodies Indiv pers Families	H 1427 H 1427 H 1427
–Ethnozoology *(May Subd Geog)*	x	H 1103	Ethnic groups	
–Etiology	x	H 1150	Diseases	
–Etymology	x	H 1154	Languages	
–Etymology–Names	x–x	H 1154	Languages	
–Euphemism	x	H 1154	Languages	
–European authors	x	H 1156	Literatures	
–European influences	x	H 1156	Literatures	H 1675
–Evacuation of civilians *(May Subd Geog)*	x	H 1200	Wars	

SUBDIVISION	SUBFIELD CODE(S)	FREE-FLOATING LIST IN SCM:SH	CATEGORY	USAGE GUIDELINES IN SCM:SH
–Evaluation	x	H 1095	see *SCM:SH*	H 1591
		H 1105	Corp bodies	H 1591
		H 1151.5	Types schools	H 1591
–Evidences, authority, etc.	x	H 1188	Sacred works	
–Evolution *(May Subd Geog)*	x	H 1147	Animals	
		H 1149	Chemicals	
		H 1164	Organs of body	
		H 1180	Plants & crops	
–Examination *(May Subd Geog)*	x	H 1164	Organs of body	
–Examinations	x	H 1095	see *SCM:SH*	
		H 1100	Classes pers	
		H 1105	Corp bodies	
		H 1110	Indiv pers	
		H 1151	Indiv schools	
		H 1151.5	Types schools	
		H 1159	Military srvces	
–Examinations–Law and legislation *(May Subd Geog)*	x–x	H 1151.5	Types schools	
–Examinations–Study guides	x–v	H 1095	see *SCM:SH*	
–Examinations–[subject]	x–x	H 1151	Indiv schools	
		H 1151.5	Types schools	
–Examinations, questions, etc.	v	H 1095	see *SCM:SH*	
		H 1100	Classes pers	
		H 1110	Indiv pers	
		H 1188	Sacred works	
–Excerpts	v	H 1095	see *SCM:SH*	
		H 1160	Musical comps	
–Excerpts, Arranged	v	H 1160	Musical comps	
–Exclamations	x	H 1154	Languages	
–Excretion	x	H 1149	Chemicals	
–Exercise *(May Subd Geog)*	x	H 1147	Animals	
–Exercise–Physiological aspects	x–x	H 1147	Animals	
–Exercise therapy *(May Subd Geog)*	x	H 1150	Diseases	

SUBDIVISION	SUBFIELD CODE(S)	FREE-FLOATING LIST IN SCM:SH	CATEGORY	USAGE GUIDELINES IN SCM:SH
–Exercises for dictation	v	H 1154	Languages	
–Exhibitions	v	H 1095	see *SCM:SH*	H 1593
–Exile *(May Subd Geog)*	x	H 1110	Indiv pers	
–Existential constructions	x	H 1154	Languages	
–Expansion and contraction *(May Subd Geog)*	x	H 1158	Materials	
–Experiments	x	H 1095	see *SCM:SH*	
–Expertising *(May Subd Geog)*	x	H 1095 H 1148	see *SCM:SH* Art	
–Explication	x	H 1156	Literatures	
–Explosion, [date]	x	H 1105	Corp bodies	
–Expulsion	x	H 1155	Legis bodies	
–Extra-canonical parallels	x	H 1188	Sacred works	
–Extrusion *(May Subd Geog)*	x	H 1158	Materials	
–Facilities	x	H 1155 H 1159	Legis bodies Military srvces	
–Facilities–Law and legislation	x–x	H 1159	Military srvces	
–Facsimiles	v	H 1095	see *SCM:SH*	H 1595
–Faculty	x	H 1151 H 1151.5	Indiv schools Types schools	
–Faculty housing	x	H 1151	Indiv schools	
–Fake books	v	H 1160	Musical comps	
–Family	x	H 1110	Indiv pers	H 1631
–Family relationships *(May Subd Geog)*	x	H 1100	Classes pers	
–Fatigue *(May Subd Geog)*	x	H 1149 H 1158	Chemicals Materials	

SUBDIVISION	SUBFIELD CODE(S)	FREE-FLOATING LIST IN SCM:SH	CATEGORY	USAGE GUIDELINES IN SCM:SH
–Feed utilization efficiency *(May Subd Geog)*	x	H 1147	Animals	
–Feeding and feeds *(May Subd Geog)*	x	H 1147	Animals	
–Feeding and feeds–Climatic factors *(May Subd Geog)*	x–x	H 1147	Animals	
–Feeding and feeds–Contamination *(May Subd Geog)*	x–x	H 1147	Animals	
–Feeding and feeds–Recipes	x–v	H 1147	Animals	
–Fees *(May Subd Geog)*	x	H 1100	Classes pers	
–Feminist criticism *(May Subd Geog)*	x	H 1188	Sacred works	
–Fenders	x	H 1195	Land vehicles	
–Fertility *(May Subd Geog)*	x	H 1147	Animals	
–Fertilization	x	H 1145.5	Bodies water	
–Fertilizers *(May Subd Geog)*	x	H 1180	Plants & crops	
–Fetuses	x	H 1147	Animals	
–Fetuses–Anatomy	x–x	H 1147	Animals	
–Fetuses–Physiology *(May Subd Geog)*	x–x	H 1147	Animals	
–Fibrosis *(May Subd Geog)*	x	H 1164	Organs of body	
–Fiction	v	H 1095	see *SCM:SH*	H 1790
		H 1100	Classes pers	H 1790
		H 1103	Ethnic groups	H 1790
		H 1105	Corp bodies	H 1790
		H 1110	Indiv pers	H 1790
		H 1120	Families	H 1790
		H 1140	Places	H 1790
–Fictional works	x	H 1110	Indiv pers	
–Field experiments	x	H 1180	Plants & crops	
–Field service	x	H 1159	Military srvces	

SUBDIVISION	SUBFIELD CODE(S)	FREE-FLOATING LIST IN SCM:SH	CATEGORY	USAGE GUIDELINES IN SCM:SH	
–Fieldwork *(May Subd Geog)*	x	H 1095	see *SCM:SH*		
–Figures of speech	x	H 1154	Languages		
–Film and video adaptations	v	H 1110	Indiv pers		
		H 1155.8	Lit works/Title		
		H 1156	Literatures		
		H 1160	Musical comps		
–Film catalogs	v	H 1095	see *SCM:SH*	H 1361	H 1670
–Films for foreign speakers	v	H 1154	Languages		
–Films for French, [Spanish, etc.] speakers	v	H 1154	Languages		
–Finance	x	H 1095	see *SCM:SH*	H 1624	
		H 1103	Ethnic groups	H 1624	
		H 1105	Corp bodies	H 1624	
		H 1151	Indiv schools	H 1624	
		H 1151.5	Types schools	H 1624	
		H 1153	Industries	H 1624	
		H 1159	Military srvces	H 1624	
		H 1187	Christian denom	H 1624	
–Finance *(May Subd Geog)*	x	H 1200	Wars		
–Finance–Law and legislation	x–x	H 1159	Military srvces		
–Finance–Law and legislation *(May Subd Geog)*	x–x	H 1103	Ethnic groups		
		H 1151.5	Types schools		
		H 1153	Industries		
–Finance, Personal	x	H 1100	Classes pers	H 1624	
		H 1103	Ethnic groups	H 1624	
		H 1110	Indiv pers	H 1624	
–Fingering	x	H 1161	Musical instrum		
–Fingering–Charts, diagrams, etc.	x–v	H 1161	Musical instrum		
–Finishing *(May Subd Geog)*	x	H 1158	Materials		
–Finishing–Waste disposal *(May Subd Geog)*	x	H 1158	Materials		
–Finishing–Waste minimization *(May Subd Geog)*	x	H 1158	Materials		

SUBDIVISION	SUBFIELD CODE(S)	FREE-FLOATING LIST IN SCM:SH	CATEGORY	USAGE GUIDELINES IN SCM:SH
–Finnish influences	x	H 1156	Literatures	H 1675
–Fire, [date]	x	H 1105	Corp bodies	
–Fire controlmen	x	H 1159	Military srvces	
–Fire fighters *(May Subd Geog)*	x	H 1200	Wars	
–Fire testing *(May Subd Geog)*	x	H 1158	Materials	
–Fire use *(May Subd Geog)*	x	H 1103	Ethnic groups	
–Firearms	x	H 1159	Military srvces	
–Firearms–Markings	x–x	H 1159	Military srvces	
–Firemen	x	H 1159	Military srvces	
–Fires and fire prevention *(May Subd Geog)*	x	H 1095 H 1153 H 1158 H 1195	see *SCM:SH* Industries Materials Land vehicles	
–Firing regulations	v	H 1159	Military srvces	
–First editions	x	H 1110 H 1156	Indiv pers Literatures	
–First editions–Bibliography	x–v	H 1110 H 1156	Indiv pers Literatures	
–First performances *(May Subd Geog)*	x	H 1160	Musical comps	
–Fishing *(May Subd Geog)*	x	H 1103	Ethnic groups	
–Flags	x	H 1159 H 1200	Military srvces Wars	
–Flammability *(May Subd Geog)*	x	H 1158	Materials	
–Flight *(May Subd Geog)*	x	H 1147	Animals	
–Flight officers	x	H 1159	Military srvces	
–Flight surgeons	x	H 1159	Military srvces	

SUBDIVISION	SUBFIELD CODE(S)	FREE-FLOATING LIST IN SCM:SH	CATEGORY	USAGE GUIDELINES IN SCM:SH
–Flowering	x	H 1180	Plants & crops	
–Flowering time	x	H 1180	Plants & crops	
–Fluid capacities *(May Subd Geog)*	x	H 1195	Land vehicles	
–Fluid dynamics	x	H 1158	Materials	
–Fluorescence *(May Subd Geog)*	x	H 1147	Animals	
–Folklore	v	H 1095	see *SCM:SH*	H 1627
		H 1100	Classes pers	H 1627
		H 1103	Ethnic groups	H 1627
		H 1140	Places	H 1627
		H 1188	Sacred works	H 1627
–Food *(May Subd Geog)*	x	H 1103	Ethnic groups	
		H 1147	Animals	
–Food service	x	H 1155	Legis bodies	
–Food service *(May Subd Geog)*	x	H 1095	see *SCM:SH*	
		H 1151.5	Types schools	
–Food supply *(May Subd Geog)*	x	H 1200	Wars	
–Football	x	H 1151	Indiv schools	
–Forced repatriation	x	H 1200	Wars	
–Forecasting	x	H 1095	see *SCM:SH*	H 1628
		H 1140	Places	H 1628
–Foreign authors	x	H 1156	Literatures	
–Foreign bodies *(May Subd Geog)*	x	H 1164	Organs of body	
–Foreign countries	z	H 1095	see *SCM:SH*	
		H 1103	Ethnic groups	H 1919.5
		H 1154	Languages	
		H 1156	Literatures	
		H 1159	Military srvces	
–Foreign countries–History and criticism	z–x	H 1156	Literatures	
–Foreign economic relations *(May Subd Geog)*	x	H 1140	Places	

SUBDIVISION	SUBFIELD CODE(S)	FREE-FLOATING LIST IN SCM:SH	CATEGORY	USAGE GUIDELINES IN SCM:SH
–Foreign elements	x	H 1154	Languages	
–Foreign elements–French, [Greek, Latin, etc.]	x–x	H 1154	Languages	
–Foreign influences	x	H 1095	see *SCM:SH*	H 1675
		H 1103	Ethnic groups	H 1675
		H 1148	Art	H 1675
		H 1156	Literatures	H 1675
–Foreign ownership	x	H 1153	Industries	
–Foreign public opinion	x	H 1140	Places	H 1955
		H 1200	Wars	H 1955
–Foreign public opinion, Austrian, [British, etc.]	x	H 1140	Places	H 1955
		H 1200	Wars	H 1955
–Foreign relations *(May Subd Geog)*	x	H 1140	Places	H 1629
		H 1187	Christian denom	H 1629
–Foreign relations–Catholic Church	x–x	H 1140	Places	H 1629
–Foreign relations–Executive agreements	x–v	H 1140	Places	
–Foreign relations–Law and legislation	x–x	H 1140	Places	
–Foreign relations–Philosophy	x–x	H 1140	Places	
–Foreign relations–Treaties	x–v	H 1140	Places	H 2227
		H 1187	Christian denom	H 2227
–Foreign relations administration	x	H 1140	Places	
–Foreign service *(May Subd Geog)*	x	H 1159	Military srvces	
–Foreign words and phrases	x	H 1154	Languages	
–Foreign words and phrases–Arabic, [Italian, etc.]	x–x	H 1154	Languages	
–Forgeries *(May Subd Geog)*	x	H 1095	see *SCM:SH*	
		H 1110	Indiv pers	
		H 1148	Art	
–Formability	x	H 1158	Materials	

SUBDIVISION	SUBFIELD CODE(S)	FREE-FLOATING LIST IN SCM:SH	CATEGORY	USAGE GUIDELINES IN SCM:SH
–Forms	v	H 1095 H 1105 H 1154.5	see *SCM:SH* Corp bodies Legal topics	
–Fracture *(May Subd Geog)*	x	H 1158	Materials	
–Fractures *(May Subd Geog)*	x	H 1147 H 1164	Animals Organs of body	
–Freedom of debate	x	H 1155	Legis bodies	
–Freemasonry	x	H 1110	Indiv pers	
–French influences	x	H 1156	Literatures	H 1675
–Freshmen	x	H 1151	Indiv schools	
–Friends and associates	x	H 1110	Indiv pers	
–Front-wheel drive	x	H 1195	Land vehicles	
–Frost damage *(May Subd Geog)*	x	H 1180	Plants & crops	
–Frost protection *(May Subd Geog)*	x	H 1180	Plants & crops	
–Frost resistance *(May Subd Geog)*	x	H 1180	Plants & crops	
–Fuel	x	H 1159	Military srvces	
–Fuel consumption	x	H 1195	Land vehicles	
–Fuel consumption–Law and legislation *(May Subd Geog)*	x–x	H 1195	Land vehicles	
–Fuel supplies	x	H 1200	Wars	
–Fuel systems	x	H 1095 H 1195	see *SCM:SH* Land vehicles	
–Fuel systems–Vapor lock	x–x	H 1195	Land vehicles	
–Fume control *(May Subd Geog)*	x	H 1095 H 1153	see *SCM:SH* Industries	
–Fumigation *(May Subd Geog)*	x	H 1180	Plants & crops	
–Function words	x	H 1154	Languages	

SUBDIVISION	SUBFIELD CODE(S)	FREE-FLOATING LIST IN SCM:SH	CATEGORY	USAGE GUIDELINES IN SCM:SH
–Funds and scholarships	x	H 1151	Indiv schools	
–Funeral customs and rites *(May Subd Geog)*	x	H 1103	Ethnic groups	
–Galician influences	x	H 1156	Literatures	H 1675
–Gallicisms	x	H 1154	Languages	
–Galvanomagnetic properties *(May Subd Geog)*	x	H 1158	Materials	
–Gambling *(May Subd Geog)*	x	H 1103	Ethnic groups	
–Games *(May Subd Geog)*	x	H 1103	Ethnic groups	
–Gas producers *(May Subd Geog)*	x	H 1195	Land vehicles	
–Gay interpretations	x	H 1180	Sacred works	
–Gays	x	H 1159	Military srvces	
–Gays *(May Subd Geog)*	x	H 1200	Wars	
–Gazetteers	v	H 1140	Places	H 1630
–Gemination	x	H 1154	Languages	
–Gender	x	H 1154	Languages	
–Gene therapy *(May Subd Geog)*	x	H 1150	Diseases	
–Genealogy	v	H 1100	Classes pers	H 1631
		H 1103	Ethnic groups	H 1631
	H	1105	Corp bodies	
		H 1140	Places	H 1631 H 1845
–Genealogy–Religious aspects	x–x	H 1140	Places	
–General staff officers	x	H 1159	Military srvces	
–Generative organs	x	H 1147	Animals	
–Genetic aspects	x	H 1150	Diseases	
–Genetic engineering *(May Subd Geog)*	x	H 1147	Animals	
		H 1180	Plants & crops	

SUBDIVISION	SUBFIELD CODE(S)	FREE-FLOATING LIST IN SCM:SH	CATEGORY	USAGE GUIDELINES IN SCM:SH
–Genetics	x	H 1147 H 1180	Animals Plants & crops	
–Genome mapping *(May Subd Geog)*	x	H 1147 H 1180	Animals Plants & crops	
–Geographic information systems *(May Subd Geog)*	x	H 1095	see *SCM:SH*	
–Geographical distribution	x	H 1147 H 1180	Animals Plants & crops	
–Geographical distribution–Climatic factors *(May Subd Geog)*	x–x	H 1147 H 1180	Animals Plants & crops	
–Geography	x	H 1140 H 1149.5 H 1188	Places Colonies Sacred works	
–German Americans	x	H 1159 H 1200	Military srvces Wars	
–German authors	x	H 1156	Literatures	
–German influences	x	H 1156	Literatures	H 1675
–Germplasm resources *(May Subd Geog)*	x	H 1147 H 1180	Animals Plants & crops	
–Germplasm resources–Catalogs and collections *(May Subd Geog)*	x–v	H 1180	Plants & crops	
–Germplasm resources–Cryopreservation *(May Subd Geog)*	x	H 1147 H 1180	Animals Plants & crops	
–Germplasm resources–Microbiology *(May Subd Geog)*	x	H 1147	Animals	
–Gerund	x	H 1154	Languages	
–Gerundive	x	H 1154	Languages	
–Gift books	v	H 1180 H 1200	Plants & crops Wars	
–Globalization	x	H 1154	Languages	

SUBDIVISION	SUBFIELD CODE(S)	FREE-FLOATING LIST IN SCM:SH	CATEGORY	USAGE GUIDELINES IN SCM:SH
–Glossaries, vocabularies, etc.	v	H 1154	Languages	H 1540 H 2184
–Glossaries, vocabularies, etc.– Polyglot	v–x	H 1154	Languages	
–Gold discoveries	x	H 1140	Places	
–Golf	x	H 1151	Indiv schools	
–Government	x	H 1154 H 1185 H 1187	Languages Religions Christian denom	
–Government jargon	x	H 1154	Languages	
–Government ownership *(May Subd Geog)*	x	H 1153	Industries	
–Government policy *(May Subd Geog)*	x	H 1095 H 1100 H 1103 H 1153	see *SCM:SH* Classes pers Ethnic groups Industries	H 1642 H 1642 H 1642 H 1642
–Government relations	x	H 1103	Ethnic groups	
–Governments in exile	x	H 1200	Wars	
–Gradation	x	H 1154	Languages	
–Grading *(May Subd Geog)*	x	H 1095 H 1147 H 1180	see *SCM:SH* Animals Plants & crops	
–Graduate students	x	H 1151	Indiv schools	
–Graduate work	x	H 1151 H 1151.5	Indiv schools Types schools	
–Graduate work–Examinations	x–x	H 1151.5	Types schools	
–Graduation requirements	x	H 1151.5	Types schools	
–Graffiti	x	H 1200	Wars	
–Grafting *(May Subd Geog)*	x	H 1180	Plants & crops	
–Grammar	x	H 1154	Languages	

SUBDIVISION	SUBFIELD CODE(S)	FREE-FLOATING LIST IN SCM:SH	CATEGORY	USAGE GUIDELINES IN SCM:SH
–Grammar–Theory, etc.	x	H 1154	Languages	
–Grammar, Comparative	x	H 1154	Languages	
–Grammar, Comparative–French, [Latin, etc.]	x–x	H 1154	Languages	
–Grammar, Generative	x	H 1154	Languages	
–Grammar, Historical	x	H 1154	Languages	
–Grammatical categories	x	H 1154	Languages	
–Grammaticalization	x	H 1154	Languages	
–Graphemics	x	H 1154	Languages	
–Graphic methods	x	H 1095	see *SCM:SH*	
–Greek authors	x	H 1156	Literatures	
–Greek influences	x	H 1156	Literatures	H 1675
–Grilles	x	H 1195	Land vehicles	
–Grooming *(May Subd Geog)*	x	H 1147	Animals	
–Ground support	x	H 1159	Military srvces	
–Growth	x	H 1147 H 1164 H 1180	Animals Organs of body Plants & crops	
–Growth–Molecular aspects	x–x	H 1164	Organs of body	
–Growth–Regulation	x–x	H 1164	Organs of body	
–Guard duty	x	H 1159	Military srvces	
–Guidebooks	v	H 1095 H 1105 H 1140	see *SCM:SH* Corp bodies Places	H 1645 H 1645
–Guided missile personnel	x	H 1159	Military srvces	
–Guided missile personnel–Training of *(May Subd Geog)*	x–x	H 1159	Military srvces	

SUBDIVISION	SUBFIELD CODE(S)	FREE-FLOATING LIST IN SCM:SH	CATEGORY	USAGE GUIDELINES IN SCM:SH
–Guided missile personnel–Training of–Aids and devices	x–x–x	H 1159	Military srvces	
–Gunners	x	H 1159	Military srvces	
–Gymnastics	x	H 1151	Indiv schools	
–Habitat *(May Subd Geog)*	x	H 1147 H 1180	Animals Plants & crops	
–Habitat–Conservation *(May Subd Geog)*	x–x	H 1147	Animals	
–Habitat suitability index models *(May Subd Geog)*	x	H 1147	Animals	
–Habitations *(May Subd Geog)*	x	H 1147	Animals	
–Hadith	x	H 1110	Indiv pers	
–Handbooks, manuals, etc.	v	H 1095 H 1100	see *SCM:SH* Classes pers	H 1646 H 1646
–Handling *(May Subd Geog)*	x	H 1147 H 1180	Animals Plants & crops	
–Handling characteristics *(May Subd Geog)*	x	H 1195	Land vehicles	
–Haplology	x	H 1154	Languages	
–Hardenability *(May Subd Geog)*	x	H 1158	Materials	
–Hardiness *(May Subd Geog)*	x	H 1180	Plants & crops	
–Harmonics	x	H 1161	Musical instrum	
–Harmonies	v	H 1188	Sacred works	
–Harmonies–History and criticism	x–x	H 1188	Sacred works	
–Harmonies, English, [French, German, etc.]	v	H 1188	Sacred works	
–Harmonies, English, [French, German, etc.]–History and criticism	x–x	H 1188	Sacred works	

SUBDIVISION	SUBFIELD CODE(S)	FREE-FLOATING LIST IN SCM:SH	CATEGORY	USAGE GUIDELINES IN SCM:SH
–Harmony	x	H 1110	Indiv pers	
–Harvesting *(May Subd Geog)*	x	H 1180	Plants & crops	
–Harvesting–Machinery *(May Subd Geog)*	x–x	H 1180	Plants & crops	
–Harvesting time *(May Subd Geog)*	x	H 1180	Plants & crops	
–Headquarters	x	H 1159	Military srvces	
–Health	x	H 1110	Indiv pers	
		H 1120	Families	
–Health *(May Subd Geog)*	x	H 1147	Animals	
		H 1180	Plants & crops	
–Health and hygiene *(May Subd Geog)*	x	H 1100	Classes pers	
		H 1103	Ethnic groups	
–Health aspects *(May Subd Geog)*	x	H 1095	see *SCM:SH*	
		H 1153	Industries	
		H 1200	Wars	
–Health promotion services *(May Subd Geog)*	x	H 1151.5	Types schools	
–Health risk assessment *(May Subd Geog)*	x	H 1100	Classes pers	
–Heat treatment *(May Subd Geog)*	x	H 1158	Materials	
–Heating *(May Subd Geog)*	x	H 1158	Materials	
–Heating and ventilation *(May Subd Geog)*	x	H 1095	see *SCM:SH*	
		H 1195	Land vehicles	
–Heating and ventilation–Control *(May Subd Geog)*	x–x	H 1095	see *SCM:SH*	
–Heian period, 794-1185	y	H 1148	Japanese art	
–Heirloom varieties *(May Subd Geog)*	x	H 1180	Plants & crops	
–Helium content *(May Subd Geog)*	x	H 1158	Materials	
–Hemorrhage *(May Subd Geog)*	x	H 1164	Organs of body	

SUBDIVISION	SUBFIELD CODE(S)	FREE-FLOATING LIST IN SCM:SH	CATEGORY	USAGE GUIDELINES IN SCM:SH
–Heraldry	x	H 1095	see *SCM:SH*	
		H 1105	Corp bodies	
–Herbarium	x	H 1105	Corp bodies	H 1427
		H 1110	Indiv pers	H 1427
		H 1120	Families	H 1427
–Herbicide injuries *(May Subd Geog)*	x	H 1180	Plants & crops	
–Hermeneutics	x	H 1188	Sacred works	
–Heteronyms	x	H 1154	Languages	
–Hiatus	x	H 1154	Languages	
–Hibernation *(May Subd Geog)*	x	H 1147	Animals	
–Hindu authors	x	H 1156	Literatures	
–Hindu interpretations	x	H 1188	Sacred works	
–Hispanic Americans	x	H 1159	Military srvces	
–Histochemistry	x	H 1164	Organs of body	
		H 1180	Plants & crops	
–Histology	x	H 1147	Animals	
		H 1164	Organs of body	
–Histopathology	x	H 1147	Animals	
		H 1150	Diseases	
		H 1164	Organs of body	
–Historical geography	x	H 1140	Places	
–Historical geography–Maps	x–v	H 1140	Places	
–Historiography	x	H 1095	see *SCM:SH*	
		H 1100	Classes pers	
		H 1103	Ethnic groups	
		H 1105	Corp bodies	
		H 1140	Places	
		H 1188	Sacred works	
		H 1200	Wars	

SUBDIVISION	SUBFIELD CODE(S)	FREE-FLOATING LIST IN SCM:SH	CATEGORY	USAGE GUIDELINES IN SCM:SH	
–History	x	H 1095	see *SCM:SH*	H 1647	H 1845
		H 1100	Classes pers	H 1647	
		H 1103	Ethnic groups	H 1647	
		H 1105	Corp bodies	H 1647	
		H 1140	Places	H 1647	H 1845
		H 1149.5	Colonies	H 1647	
		H 1154	Languages	H 1647	
		H 1159	Military srvces	H 1647	
		H 1187	Christian denom	H 1647	
		H 1188	Sacred works	H 1647	
–History–[period subdivision]– Biography	x–y–v	H 1140	Places		
–History–[period subdivision]– Biography–Anecdotes	x–y–v–v	H 1140	Places		
–History–[period subdivision]– Biography–Portraits	x–y–v–v	H 1140	Places		
–History–[period subdivision]– Biography–Sources	x–y–x–v	H 1140	Places		
–History–[period subdivision]– Chronology	x–y–v	H 1140	Places		
–History–[period subdivision]– Historiography	x–y–x	H 1140	Places		
–History–[period subdivision]– Philosophy	x–y–x	H 1140	Places		
–History–[period subdivision]– Sources	x–y–v	H 1140	Places		
–History–To 1500	x–y	H 1095	see *SCM:SH*	H 1647	
–History–Modern period, 1500-	x–y	H 1187	Christian denom		
–History–16th century	x–y	H 1095	see *SCM:SH*	H 1647	
		H 1100	Classes pers	H 1647	
		H 1103	Ethnic groups	H 1647	
		H 1105	Corp bodies	H 1647	
		H 1140	Places	H 1647	
		H 1159	Military srvces	H 1647	
		H 1187	Christian denom	H 1647	

SUBDIVISION	SUBFIELD CODE(S)	FREE-FLOATING LIST IN SCM:SH	CATEGORY	USAGE GUIDELINES IN SCM:SH
–History–17th century	x–y	H 1095	see *SCM:SH*	H 1647
		H 1100	Classes pers	H 1647
		H 1103	Ethnic groups	H 1647
		H 1105	Corp bodies	H 1647
		H 1140	Places	H 1647
		H 1159	Military srvces	H 1647
		H 1187	Christian denom	H 1647
–History–18th century	x–y	H 1095	see *SCM:SH*	H 1647
		H 1100	Classes pers	H 1647
		H 1103	Ethnic groups	H 1647
		H 1105	Corp bodies	H 1647
		H 1140	Places	H 1647
		H 1159	Military srvces	H 1647
		H 1187	Christian denom	H 1647
–History–Revolution, 1775-1783, [War of 1812, etc.]	x–y	H 1159	Military srvces	
–History–19th century	x–y	H 1095	see *SCM:SH*	H 1647
		H 1100	Classes pers	H 1647
		H 1103	Ethnic groups	H 1647
		H 1105	Corp bodies	H 1647
		H 1140	Places	H 1647
		H 1159	Military srvces	H 1647
		H 1187	Christian denom	H 1647
–History–20th century	x–y	H 1095	see *SCM:SH*	H 1647
		H 1100	Classes pers	H 1647
		H 1103	Ethnic groups	H 1647
		H 1105	Corp bodies	H 1647
		H 1140	Places	H 1647
		H 1159	Military srvces	H 1647
		H 1187	Christian denom	H 1647
–History–21st century	x–y	H 1095	see *SCM:SH*	H 1647
		H 1100	Classes pers	H 1647
		H 1103	Ethnic groups	H 1647
		H 1105	Corp bodies	H 1647
		H 1140	Places	H 1647
		H 1159	Military srvces	H 1647
		H 1187	Christian denom	H 1647
–History–1965-	x–y	H 1187	Christian denom	H 1647
–History–Anecdotes	x–v	H 1140	Places	

SUBDIVISION	SUBFIELD CODE(S)	FREE-FLOATING LIST IN SCM:SH	CATEGORY	USAGE GUIDELINES IN SCM:SH	
–History–Autonomy and independence movements	x–x	H 1140	Places		
–History–Chronology	x–v	H 1095	see *SCM:SH*	H 1367	
		H 1103	Ethnic groups	H 1367	
		H 1105	Corp bodies	H 1367	
		H 1140	Places	H 1367	
		H 1159	Military srvces	H 1367	
–History–Comic books, strips, etc.	x–v	H 1140	Places		
–History–Errors, inventions, etc.	x–x	H 1140	Places		
–History–Humor	x–v	H 1140	Places		
–History–Periodization	x–x	H 1140	Places		
–History–Philosophy	x–x	H 1095	see *SCM:SH*		
		H 1140	Places		
–History–Pictorial works	x–v	H 1140	Places		
–History–Prophecies	x–x	H 1140	Places		
–History–Religious aspects	x–x	H 1140	Places		
–History–Religious aspects– Baptists, [Catholic Church, etc.]	x–x–x	H 1140	Places		
–History–Religious aspects– Buddhism, [Christianity, etc.]	x–x–x	H 1140	Places		
–History–Sources	x–v	H 1095	see *SCM:SH*	H 1647	H 2080
		H 1100	Classes pers	H 1647	H 2080
		H 1103	Ethnic groups	H 1647	H 2080
		H 1105	Corp bodies	H 1647	H 2080
		H 1140	Places	H 1647	H 2080
–History, Local	x	H 1140	Places		
–History, Local–Collectibles	x–x	H 1140	Places		
–History, Military	x	H 1140	Places		
–History, Military–16th century	x–y	H 1140	Places		
–History, Military–17th century	x–y	H 1140	Places		

SUBDIVISION	SUBFIELD CODE(S)	FREE-FLOATING LIST IN SCM:SH	CATEGORY	USAGE GUIDELINES IN SCM:SH
–History, Military–18th century	x–y	H 1140	Places	
–History, Military–19th century	x–y	H 1140	Places	
–History, Military–20th century	x–y	H 1140	Places	
–History, Military–21st century	x–y	H 1140	Places	
–History, Military–Religious aspects	x–x	H 1140	Places	
–History, Naval	x	H 1140	Places	
–History, Naval–16th century	x–y	H 1140	Places	
–History, Naval–17th century	x–y	H 1140	Places	
–History, Naval–18th century	x–y	H 1140	Places	
–History, Naval–19th century	x–y	H 1140	Places	
–History, Naval–20th century	x–y	H 1140	Places	
–History, Naval–21st century	x–y	H 1140	Places	
–History and criticism	x	H 1095 H 1156 H 1160	see *SCM:SH* Literatures Musical comps	H 1647 H 1790 H 2190
–History and criticism–Theory, etc.	x–x	H 1156	Literatures	
–History of Biblical events	x	H 1188	Sacred works	
–History of Biblical events–Art	x–v	H 1188	Sacred works	
–History of contemporary events	x	H 1188	Sacred works	
–History of doctrines	x	H 1095	see *SCM:SH*	
–History of doctrines–Early church, ca. 30-600	x–y	H 1095	see *SCM:SH*	
–History of doctrines–Middle Ages, 600-1500	x–y	H 1095	see *SCM:SH*	
–History of doctrines–16th century	x–y	H 1095	see *SCM:SH*	

SUBDIVISION	SUBFIELD CODE(S)	FREE-FLOATING LIST IN SCM:SH	CATEGORY	USAGE GUIDELINES IN SCM:SH
–History of doctrines–17th century	x–y	H 1095	see *SCM:SH*	
–History of doctrines–18th century	x–y	H 1095	see *SCM:SH*	
–History of doctrines–19th century	x–y	H 1095	see *SCM:SH*	
–History of doctrines–20th century	x–y	H 1095	see *SCM:SH*	
–History of doctrines–21st century	x–y	H 1095	see *SCM:SH*	
–Hockey	x	H 1151	Indiv schools	
–Home care *(May Subd Geog)*	x	H 1100 H 1103	Classes pers Ethnic groups	
–Home range *(May Subd Geog)*	x	H 1147	Animals	
–Homeopathic treatment *(May Subd Geog)*	x	H 1150	Diseases	
–Homes and haunts *(May Subd Geog)*	x	H 1100 H 1103 H 1105 H 1110 H 1120	Classes pers Ethnic groups Corp bodies Indiv pers Families	H 1334
–Homiletical use	x	H 1188	Sacred works	
–Homing *(May Subd Geog)*	x	H 1147	Animals	
–Homonyms	x	H 1154	Languages	
–Honor system	x	H 1151	Indiv schools	
–Honorific	x	H 1154	Languages	
–Honorific unit titles	x	H 1159	Military srvces	
–Honors courses *(May Subd Geog)*	x	H 1151.5	Types schools	
–Hormone therapy *(May Subd Geog)*	x	H 1150	Diseases	
–Hormone therapy–Complications *(May Subd Geog)*	x–x	H 1150	Diseases	
–Horns	x	H 1195	Land vehicles	

SUBDIVISION	SUBFIELD CODE(S)	FREE-FLOATING LIST IN SCM:SH	CATEGORY	USAGE GUIDELINES IN SCM:SH
–Hospice care *(May Subd Geog)*	x	H 1100 H 1103	Classes pers Ethnic groups	
–Hospital care *(May Subd Geog)*	x	H 1100 H 1103	Classes pers Ethnic groups	
–Hospital ships	x	H 1159	Military srvces	
–Hospitals *(May Subd Geog)*	x	H 1100 H 1103 H 1150 H 1200	Classes pers Ethnic groups Diseases Wars	
–Host plants *(May Subd Geog)*	x	H 1147	Animals	
–Hostages *(May Subd Geog)*	x	H 1200	Wars	
–Hot weather conditions *(May Subd Geog)*	x	H 1095	see *SCM:SH*	
–Hot working *(May Subd Geog)*	x	H 1158	Materials	
–Housing *(May Subd Geog)*	x	H 1100 H 1103 H 1147	Classes pers Ethnic groups Animals	
–Housing–Air conditioning *(May Subd Geog)*	x–x	H 1147	Animals	
–Housing–Decoration *(May Subd Geog)*	x–x	H 1147	Animals	
–Housing–Design and construction	x–x	H 1147	Animals	
–Housing–Disinfection *(May Subd Geog)*	x–x	H 1147	Animals	
–Housing–Environmental engineering *(May Subd Geog)*	x–x	H 1147	Animals	
–Housing–Heating and ventilation *(May Subd Geog)*	x–x	H 1147	Animals	
–Housing–Insulation *(May Subd Geog)*	x–x	H 1147	Animals	
–Housing–Lighting *(May Subd Geog)*	x–x	H 1147	Animals	

SUBDIVISION	SUBFIELD CODE(S)	FREE-FLOATING LIST IN SCM:SH	CATEGORY	USAGE GUIDELINES IN SCM:SH
–Housing–Odor control *(May Subd Geog)*	x–x	H 1147	Animals	
–Housing–Safety measures	x–x	H 1147	Animals	
–Housing–Sanitation *(May Subd Geog)*	x–x	H 1147	Animals	
–Housing–Specifications *(May Subd Geog)*	x–v	H 1147	Animals	
–Housing–Waste disposal *(May Subd Geog)*	x–x	H 1147	Animals	
–Humor	v	H 1095	see *SCM:SH*	
		H 1100	Classes pers	
		H 1103	Ethnic groups	
		H 1105	Corp bodies	
		H 1110	Indiv pers	
		H 1140	Places	
		H 1188	Sacred works	
–Hungarian influences	x	H 1156	Literatures	H 1675
–Hunting *(May Subd Geog)*	x	H 1103	Ethnic groups	
–Hurricane effects *(May Subd Geog)*	x	H 1095	see *SCM:SH*	
–Husking *(May Subd Geog)*	x	H 1180	Plants & crops	
–Hybridization *(May Subd Geog)*	x	H 1147	Animals	
		H 1180	Plants & crops	
–Hydatids *(May Subd Geog)*	x	H 1164	Organs of body	
–Hydraulic equipment	x	H 1195	Land vehicles	
–Hydrogen content *(May Subd Geog)*	x	H 1158	Materials	
–Hydrogen embrittlement	x	H 1158	Materials	
–Hymns	v	H 1187	Christian denom	
–Hymns–History and criticism	x–x	H 1187	Christian denom	
–Hymns–Texts	v–v	H 1187	Christian denom	
–Hypertrophy *(May Subd Geog)*	x	H 1164	Organs of body	

SUBDIVISION	SUBFIELD CODE(S)	FREE-FLOATING LIST IN SCM:SH	CATEGORY	USAGE GUIDELINES IN SCM:SH
–Ice breaking operations	x	H 1159	Military srvces	
–Identification	x	H 1095	see *SCM:SH*	
		H 1100	Classes pers	
–Identification	v	H 1095	see *SCM:SH*	
		H 1147	Animals	
		H 1180	Plants & crops	
–Ideophone	x	H 1154	Languages	
–Idioms	x	H 1154	Languages	
–Ignition	x	H 1195	Land vehicles	
–Ignition–Electronic systems	x–x	H 1195	Land vehicles	
–Illustrations	v	H 1095	see *SCM:SH*	H 1659
		H 1110	Indiv pers	H 1659
		H 1155.6	Lit works/Auth	H 1659
		H 1155.8	Lit works/Title	H 1659
		H 1156	Literatures	H 1659
		H 1188	Sacred works	H 1659
–Imaging *(May Subd Geog)*	x	H 1150	Diseases	
		H 1164	Organs of body	
–Immunodiagnosis *(May Subd Geog)*	x	H 1150	Diseases	
–Immunological aspects	x	H 1150	Diseases	
–Immunology	x	H 1147	Animals	
		H 1149	Chemicals	
		H 1164	Organs of body	
–Immunology–Genetic aspects	x–x	H 1147	Animals	
–Immunotherapy *(May Subd Geog)*	x	H 1150	Diseases	
–Impact testing *(May Subd Geog)*	x	H 1158	Materials	
–Impeachment	x	H 1110	Indiv pers	
–Imperative	x	H 1154	Languages	
–Implements *(May Subd Geog)*	x	H 1103	Ethnic groups	
–Imprints	v	H 1140	Places	H 1660

SUBDIVISION	SUBFIELD CODE(S)	FREE-FLOATING LIST IN SCM:SH	CATEGORY	USAGE GUIDELINES IN SCM:SH	
–Imprisonment	x	H 1110	Indiv pers		
–In art	v	H 1095	see *SCM:SH*	H 362	H 910
		H 1105	Corp bodies	H 362	
		H 1140	Places	H 362	H 910
		H 1187	Christian denom	H 362	
–In bookplates	x	H 1105	Corp bodies		
		H 1110	Indiv pers		
		H 1140	Places		
		H 1200	Wars		
–In literature	x	H 1105	Corp bodies	H 362	
		H 1110	Indiv pers	H 362	
		H 1120	Families	H 362	
		H 1140	Places	H 362	H 910
		H 1187	Christian denom	H 362	
		H 1188	Sacred works	H 362	
–In mass media	x	H 1105	Corp bodies		
		H 1110	Indiv pers		
		H 1120	Families		
		H 1140	Places	H 910	
–In motion pictures	x	H 1105	Corp bodies		
		H 1110	Indiv pers		
		H 1120	Families		
		H 1140	Places	H 910	
		H 1187	Christian denom		
–In opera	x	H 1110	Indiv pers		
–In popular culture	x	H 1140	Places		
–In-service training *(May Subd Geog)*	x	H 1100	Classes pers		
–Inauguration, [date]	x	H 1110	Indiv pers		
–Inclusions *(May Subd Geog)*	x	H 1158	Materials		
–Indeclinable words	x	H 1154	Languages		
–Index maps	v	H 1140	Places		
–Indexes	v	H 1095	see *SCM:SH*	H 1670	
–Indian influences	x	H 1156	Literatures	H 1675	

SUBDIVISION	SUBFIELD CODE(S)	FREE-FLOATING LIST IN SCM:SH	CATEGORY	USAGE GUIDELINES IN SCM:SH
–Indian troops	x	H 1159	Military srvces	
–Indians	x	H 1159	Military srvces	
		H 1200	Wars	
–Indic influences	x	H 1156	Literatures	H 1675
–Indicative	x	H 1154	Languages	
–Indirect discourse	x	H 1154	Languages	
–Indirect object	x	H 1154	Languages	
–Induced spawning *(May Subd Geog)*	x	H 1147	Animals	
–Industrial applications *(May Subd Geog)*	x	H 1095	see *SCM:SH*	
		H 1149	Chemicals	
		H 1180	Plants & crops	
–Industrial capacity *(May Subd Geog)*	x	H 1153	Industries	
–Industries *(May Subd Geog)*	x	H 1103	Ethnic groups	
–Infallibility	x	H 1187	Christian denom	
–Infancy *(May Subd Geog)*	x	H 1147	Animals	
–Infantry	x	H 1159	Military srvces	
–Infantry–Drill and tactics	x–x	H 1159	Military srvces	
–Infections *(May Subd Geog)*	x	H 1147	Animals	
		H 1164	Organs of body	
–Infertility *(May Subd Geog)*	x	H 1147	Animals	
–Infinitival constructions	x	H 1154	Languages	
–Infinitive	x	H 1154	Languages	
–Infixes	x	H 1154	Languages	
–Inflection	x	H 1154	Languages	

SUBDIVISION	SUBFIELD CODE(S)	FREE-FLOATING LIST IN SCM:SH	CATEGORY	USAGE GUIDELINES IN SCM:SH
–Influence	x	H 1095	see *SCM:SH*	H 1675
		H 1105	Corp bodies	H 1675
		H 1110	Indiv pers	H 1675
		H 1148	Art	H 1675
		H 1155.8	Lit works/Title	H 1675
		H 1185	Religions	H 1675
		H 1187	Christian denom	H 1675
		H 1188	Sacred works	H 1675
		H 1200	Wars	H 1675
–Influence–Medieval civilization	x–x	H 1188	Sacred works	
–Influence–Modern civilization	x–x	H 1188	Sacred works	
–Influence–Slavic civilization	x–x	H 1188	Sacred works	
–Influence–Western civilization	x–x	H 1188	Sacred works	
–Influence on French, [Italian, etc.]	x	H 1154	Languages	
–Influence on foreign languages	x	H 1154	Languages	
–Information resources	x	H 1095	see *SCM:SH*	
–Information resources management *(May Subd Geog)*	x	H 1095	see *SCM:SH*	
		H 1105	Corp bodies	
		H 1153	Industries	
–Information services	x	H 1095	see *SCM:SH*	H 1675.5
		H 1100	Classes pers	H 1675.5
		H 1103	Ethnic groups	H 1675.5
		H 1105	Corp bodies	H 1675.5
		H 1110	Indiv pers	H 1675.5
		H 1140	Places	H 1675.5
		H 1153	Industries	H 1675.5
–Information services–Law and legislation *(May Subd Geog)*	x–x	H 1153	Industries	
–Information technology	x	H 1105	Corp bodies	
–Information technology *(May Subd Geog)*	x	H 1095	see *SCM:SH*	
		H 1153	Industries	
–Inhibitors	x	H 1149	Chemicals	
–Innervation	x	H 1164	Organs of body	

SUBDIVISION	SUBFIELD CODE(S)	FREE-FLOATING LIST IN SCM:SH	CATEGORY	USAGE GUIDELINES IN SCM:SH
–Inoculation *(May Subd Geog)*	x	H 1180	Plants & crops	
–Insect resistance *(May Subd Geog)*	x	H 1180	Plants & crops	
–Insect resistance–Genetic aspects	x–x	H 1180	Plants & crops	
–Insignia	x	H 1095	see *SCM:SH*	
		H 1105	Corp bodies	
		H 1151.5	Types schools	
		H 1159	Military srvces	
–Inspection	x	H 1159	Military srvces	
–Inspection *(May Subd Geog)*	x	H 1095	see *SCM:SH*	H 1676.5
		H 1147	Animals	
		H 1180	Plants & crops	
		H 1195	Land vehicles	
–Inspiration	x	H 1188	Sacred works	
–Installation *(May Subd Geog)*	x	H 1095	see *SCM:SH*	
–Institutional care *(May Subd Geog)*	x	H 1100	Classes pers	
		H 1103	Ethnic groups	
–Instruction and study *(May Subd Geog)*	x	H 1160	Musical comps	H 2110
		H 1161	Musical instrum	H 2110
–Instruction and study–Juvenile	x–v	H 1160	Musical comps	
		H 1161	Musical instrum	
–Instructive editions	v	H 1160	Musical comps	
–Instrument panels	x	H 1195	Land vehicles	
–Instrument panels–Padding	x–x	H 1195	Land vehicles	
–Instrumental settings	v	H 1160	Musical comps	
–Instruments	x	H 1095	see *SCM:SH*	
		H 1195	Land vehicles	
–Instruments–Display systems	x–x	H 1195	Land vehicles	
–Insurance *(May Subd Geog)*	x	H 1153	Industries	
–Insurance–Law and legislation *(May Subd Geog)*	x–x	H 1153	Industries	

SUBDIVISION	SUBFIELD CODE(S)	FREE-FLOATING LIST IN SCM:SH	CATEGORY	USAGE GUIDELINES IN SCM:SH
–Insurance requirements *(May Subd Geog)*	x	H 1100	Classes pers	
–Integrated control *(May Subd Geog)*	x	H 1147 H 1180	Animals Plants & crops	
–Intellectual life	x	H 1100 H 1103 H 1140	Classes pers Ethnic groups Places	
–Intellectual life–16th century	x–y	H 1100 H 1103 H 1140	Classes pers Ethnic groups Places	
–Intellectual life–17th century	x–y	H 1100 H 1103 H 1140	Classes pers Ethnic groups Places	
–Intellectual life–18th century	x–y	H 1100 H 1103 H 1140	Classes pers Ethnic groups Places	
–Intellectual life–19th century	x–y	H 1100 H 1103 H 1140	Classes pers Ethnic groups Places	
–Intellectual life–20th century	x–y	H 1100 H 1103 H 1140	Classes pers Ethnic groups Places	
–Intellectual life–21st century	x–y	H 1100 H 1103 H 1140	Classes pers Ethnic groups Places	
–Intelligence levels *(May Subd Geog)*	x	H 1100 H 1103	Classes pers Ethnic groups	
–Intelligence specialists	x	H 1159	Military srvces	
–Intelligence testing *(May Subd Geog)*	x	H 1100 H 1103	Classes pers Ethnic groups	
–Intensification	x	H 1154	Languages	
–Interactive multimedia	v	H 1095	see *SCM:SH*	
–Interiors *(May Subd Geog)*	x	H 1195	Land vehicles	

SUBDIVISION	SUBFIELD CODE(S)	FREE-FLOATING LIST IN SCM:SH	CATEGORY	USAGE GUIDELINES IN SCM:SH
–Interjections	x	H 1154	Languages	
–Interlinear translations	v	H 1188	Sacred works	
–Interlinear translations, English, [French, etc.]	v	H 1188	Sacred works	
–Intermediate care *(May Subd Geog)*	x	H 1100	Classes pers	
–International cooperation	x	H 1095	see *SCM:SH*	
–International status	x	H 1140	Places	
–Internet marketing *(May Subd Geog)*	x	H 1095	see *SCM:SH*	
–Interpretation	x	H 1095	see *SCM:SH*	
–Interpretation (Phrasing, dynamics, etc.)	x	H 1160	Musical comps	
–Interpretation and construction	x	H 1154.5	Legal topics	
–Interrogative	x	H 1154	Languages	
–Interventional radiology *(May Subd Geog)*	x	H 1150 H 1164	Diseases Organs of body	
–Interviews	v	H 1100 H 1103 H 1105 H 1110	Classes pers Ethnic groups Corp bodies Indiv pers	H 1678 H 1678 H 1678 H 1678
–Intonation	x	H 1154 H 1161	Languages Musical instrum	
–Intraoperative radiotherapy *(May Subd Geog)*	x	H 1150	Diseases	
–Introductions	v	H 1188	Sacred works	
–Inventories	v	H 1095 H 1153	see *SCM:SH* Industries	
–Inventory control	x	H 1105 H 1159	Corp bodies Military srvces	

SUBDIVISION	SUBFIELD CODE(S)	FREE-FLOATING LIST IN SCM:SH	CATEGORY	USAGE GUIDELINES IN SCM:SH
–Inventory control *(May Subd Geog)*	x	H 1095 H 1153	see *SCM:SH* Industries	
–Iranian influences	x	H 1156	Literatures	H 1675
–Irish Americans	x	H 1159	Military srvces	
–Irish authors	x	H 1156	Literatures	
–Irish influences	x	H 1156	Literatures	H 1675
–Irrigation *(May Subd Geog)*	x	H 1180	Plants & crops	
–Islamic influences	x	H 1156	Literatures	H 1675
–Islamic interpretations	x	H 1188	Sacred works	
–Isotopes *(May Subd Geog)*	x	H 1149	Chemicals	
–Isotopes–Half-life *(May Subd Geog)*	x	H 1149	Chemicals	
–Italian Americans	x	H 1159 H 1200	Military services Wars	
–Italian authors	x	H 1156	Literatures	
–Italian influences	x	H 1156	Literatures	H 1675
–Jaina authors	x	H 1156	Literatures	
–Japanese Americans	x	H 1159 H 1200	Military srvces Wars	
–Japanese authors	x	H 1156	Literatures	
–Japanese influences	x	H 1156	Literatures	H 1675
–Jargon	x	H 1154	Languages	
–Jewelry *(May Subd Geog)*	x	H 1103	Ethnic groups	
–Jewish authors	x	H 1156	Literatures	
–Jewish Christian authors	x	H 1156	Literatures	
–Jews *(May Subd Geog)*	x	H 1200	Wars	

SUBDIVISION	SUBFIELD CODE(S)	FREE-FLOATING LIST IN SCM:SH	CATEGORY	USAGE GUIDELINES IN SCM:SH
–Job descriptions	v	H 1105	Corp bodies	
		H 1159	Military srvces	
–Job descriptions (May Subd Geog)	v	H 1095	see SCM:SH	
		H 1100	Classes pers	
–Job satisfaction (May Subd Geog)	x	H 1100	Classes pers	
–Job stress (May Subd Geog)	x	H 1100	Classes pers	
		H 1103	Ethnic groups	
–Job vacancies (May Subd Geog)	x	H 1153	Industries	
–Journalism, Military (May Subd Geog)	x	H 1200	Wars	
–Journalists	x	H 1159	Military srvces	
		H 1200	Wars	
–Judging (May Subd Geog)	x	H 1147	Animals	
		H 1180	Plants & crops	
–Jungle warfare	x	H 1200	Wars	
–Juvenile	v	H 1160	Musical comps	
–Juvenile drama	v	H 1095	see SCM:SH	H 1690
		H 1100	Classes pers	H 1690
		H 1103	Ethnic groups	H 1690
		H 1105	Corp bodies	H 1690
		H 1110	Indiv pers	H 1690
		H 1140	Places	H 1690
–Juvenile fiction	v	H 1095	see SCM:SH	H 1690
		H 1100	Classes pers	H 1690
		H 1103	Ethnic groups	H 1690
		H 1105	Corp bodies	H 1690
		H 1110	Indiv pers	H 1690
		H 1140	Places	H 1690
–Juvenile films	v	H 1095	see SCM:SH	H 1690

SUBDIVISION	SUBFIELD CODE(S)	FREE-FLOATING LIST IN SCM:SH	CATEGORY	USAGE GUIDELINES IN SCM:SH
–Juvenile humor	v	H 1095	see *SCM:SH*	H 1690
		H 1100	Classes pers	H 1690
		H 1103	Ethnic groups	H 1690
		H 1105	Corp bodies	H 1690
		H 1110	Indiv pers	H 1690
		H 1140	Places	H 1690
		H 1188	Sacred works	H 1690
–Juvenile literature	v	H 1095	see *SCM:SH*	H 1690
–Juvenile poetry	v	H 1095	see *SCM:SH*	H 1690
		H 1100	Classes pers	H 1690
		H 1103	Ethnic groups	H 1690
		H 1105	Corp bodies	H 1690
		H 1110	Indiv pers	H 1690
		H 1140	Places	H 1690
		H 1188	Sacred works	H 1690
–Juvenile software	v	H 1095	see *SCM:SH*	H 2070
–Juvenile sound recordings	v	H 1095	see *SCM:SH*	H 1690
–Kamakura-Momoyama periods, 1185-1600	y	H 1148	Japanese art	
–Kidnapping, [date]	x	H 1110	Indiv pers	
–Kings and rulers	x	H 1103	Ethnic groups	
		H 1140	Places	H 1574
–Kings and rulers–Abdication	x–x	H 1140	Places	
–Kings and rulers–Art patronage	x–x	H 1140	Places	
–Kings and rulers–Assassination	x–x	H 1103	Ethnic groups	
		H 1140	Places	
–Kings and rulers–Brothers	x–x	H 1140	Places	
–Kings and rulers–Children	x–x	H 1103	Ethnic groups	
		H 1140	Places	
–Kings and rulers–Death and burial	x–x	H 1103	Ethnic groups	
		H 1140	Places	
–Kings and rulers–Deposition	x–x	H 1140	Places	
–Kings and rulers–Dwellings	x–x	H 1140	Places	

SUBDIVISION	SUBFIELD CODE(S)	FREE-FLOATING LIST IN SCM:SH	CATEGORY	USAGE GUIDELINES IN SCM:SH
–Kings and rulers–Education	x–x	H 1103 H 1140	Ethnic groups Places	
–Kings and rulers–Folklore	x–v	H 1103 H 1140	Ethnic groups Places	
–Kings and rulers–Genealogy	x–v	H 1103 H 1140	Ethnic groups Places	
–Kings and rulers–Heraldry	x–x	H 1140	Places	
–Kings and rulers–Mythology	x–x	H 1103 H 1140	Ethnic groups Places	
–Kings and rulers–Paramours	x–x	H 1140	Places	
–Kings and rulers–Religious aspects	x–x	H 1103 H 1140	Ethnic groups Places	
–Kings and rulers–Sisters	x–x	H 1140	Places	
–Kings and rulers–Succession	x–x	H 1103 H 1140	Ethnic groups Places	
–Kings and rulers–Tombs	x–x	H 1140	Places	
–Kings and rulers–Travel *(May Subd Geog)*	x–x	H 1140	Places	
–Kinship *(May Subd Geog)*	x	H 1103	Ethnic groups	
–Knowledge–Agriculture, [America, etc.]	x	H 1110	Indiv pers	
–Knowledge and learning	x	H 1110	Indiv pers	
–Koranic teaching	x	H 1095	see *SCM:SH*	
–Korean authors	x	H 1156	Literatures	
–Koryŏ period, 935-1392	y	H 1148	Korean art	
–Kurdish authors	x	H 1156	Literatures	
–Kyrgyz authors	x	H 1156	Literatures	
–Labeling *(May Subd Geog)*	x	H 1095	see *SCM:SH*	

SUBDIVISION	SUBFIELD CODE(S)	FREE-FLOATING LIST IN SCM:SH	CATEGORY	USAGE GUIDELINES IN SCM:SH
–Labiality	x	H 1154	Languages	
–Labor productivity *(May Subd Geog)*	x	H 1095 H 1153	see *SCM:SH* Industries	
–Labor unions *(May Subd Geog)*	x	H 1100	Classes pers	
–Labor unions–Organizing *(May Subd Geog)*	x–x	H 1100	Classes pers	
–Laboratory manuals	v	H 1095	see *SCM:SH*	H 1646
–Land tenure *(May Subd Geog)*	x	H 1103	Ethnic groups	
–Landscape architecture *(May Subd Geog)*	x	H 1095	see *SCM:SH*	
–Language	x	H 1095 H 1100 H 1105 H 1110 H 1151 H 1154.5 H 1155.8 H 1200	see *SCM:SH* Classes pers Corp bodies Indiv pers Indiv schools Legal topics Lit works/Title Wars	
–Language–Glossaries, etc.	x–v	H 1110 H 1155.8	Indiv pers Lit works/Title	
–Language, style	x	H 1188	Sacred works	
–Languages	x	H 1103 H 1140	Ethnic groups Places	
–Languages–Law and legislation	x–x	H 1140	Places	
–Languages–Political aspects	x–x	H 1140	Places	
–Languages–Texts	x–v	H 1103 H 1140	Ethnic groups Places	
–Larvae *(May Subd Geog)*	x	H 1147	Animals	
–Larvae–Dispersal *(May Subd Geog)*	x–x	H 1147	Animals	
–Larvae–Ecology *(May Subd Geog)*	x–x	H 1147	Animals	

SUBDIVISION	SUBFIELD CODE(S)	FREE-FLOATING LIST IN SCM:SH	CATEGORY	USAGE GUIDELINES IN SCM:SH
–Larvae–Effect of ultraviolet radiation on *(May Subd Geog)*	x–x	H 1147	Animals	
–Larvae–Endocrinology	x–x	H 1147	Animals	
–Larvae–Food *(May Subd Geog)*	x–x	H 1147	Animals	
–Larvae–Geographical distribution	x–x	H 1147	Animals	
–Larvae–Microbiology *(May Subd Geog)*	x–x	H 1147	Animals	
–Laser surgery *(May Subd Geog)*	x	H 1164 H 1150	Organs of body Diseases	
–Laser surgery–Instruments	x	H 1164	Organs of body	
–Last years	x	H 1110	Indiv pers	
–Lateral stability	x	H 1195	Land vehicles	
–Latin American influences	x	H 1156	Literatures	H 1675
–Law and legislation *(May Subd Geog)*	x	H 1147 H 1149 H 1150 H 1151.5 H 1153 H 1158 H 1180 H 1195 H 1200	Animals Chemicals Diseases Types schools Industries Materials Plants & crops Land vehicles Wars	H 1705 H 1705 H 1705 H 1705 H 1705 H 1705 H 1705 H 1705 H 1705
–Lawyers	x	H 1159	Military srvces	
–Lead content *(May Subd Geog)*	x	H 1149	Chemicals	
–Lead sheets	v	H 1160	Musical comps	
–Leadership	x	H 1155	Legis bodies	
–Leaves and furloughs	x	H 1159	Military srvces	
–Legal research	x	H 1154.5	Legal topics	H 1710
–Legal status, laws, etc. *(May Subd Geog)*	x	H 1100 H 1103	Classes pers Ethnic groups	H 1705 H 1705

SUBDIVISION	SUBFIELD CODE(S)	FREE-FLOATING LIST IN SCM:SH	CATEGORY	USAGE GUIDELINES IN SCM:SH	
–Legends	v	H 1095	see *SCM:SH*	H 1627	H 1795
		H 1110	Indiv pers	H 1627	H 1795
		H 1188	Sacred works	H 1627	H 1795
–Legislative history	x	H 1154.5	Legal topics		
–Lexicography	x	H 1154	Languages		
		H 1185	Religions		
–Lexicology	x	H 1154	Languages		
–Lexicology, Historical	x	H 1154	Languages		
–Libraries	x	H 1105	Corp bodies		
		H 1200	Wars		
–Library	x	H 1105	Corp bodies	H 1427	H 1361
		H 1110	Indiv pers	H 1427	H 1361
		H 1120	Families	H 1427	H 1361
–Library–Marginal notes	x–v	H 1110	Indiv pers		
–Library–Microform catalogs	x–v	H 1110	Indiv pers		
–Library resources	x	H 1095	see *SCM:SH*		
		H 1100	Classes pers		
		H 1103	Ethnic groups		
		H 1105	Corp bodies		
		H 1110	Indiv pers		
		H 1140	Places		
–Librettos	v	H 1160	Musical comps		
–Licenses *(May Subd Geog)*	x	H 1095	see *SCM:SH*		
		H 1100	Classes pers		
		H 1153	Industries		
		H 1195	Land vehicles		
–Licenses–Fees *(May Subd Geog)*	x–x	H 1095	see *SCM:SH*		
		H 1100	Classes pers		
		H 1153	Industries		
		H 1195	Land vehicles		
–Life cycles *(May Subd Geog)*	x	H 1147	Animals		
		H 1180	Plants & crops		
–Life skills assessment *(May Subd Geog)*	x	H 1100	Classes pers		
		H 1103	Ethnic groups		

SUBDIVISION	SUBFIELD CODE(S)	FREE-FLOATING LIST IN SCM:SH	CATEGORY	USAGE GUIDELINES IN SCM:SH
–Life skills guides	v	H 1100	Classes pers	
		H 1103	Ethnic groups	
–Lighting *(May Subd Geog)*	x	H 1095	see *SCM:SH*	
		H 1195	Land vehicles	
–Lighting–Law and legislation *(May Subd Geog)*	x–x	H 1195	Land vehicles	
–Linear programming	x	H 1095	see *SCM:SH*	
–Lists of vessels	v	H 1159	Military srvces	
–Literary art	x	H 1110	Indiv pers	
–Literary collections	v	H 1095	see *SCM:SH*	
		H 1100	Classes pers	
		H 1103	Ethnic groups	
		H 1105	Corp bodies	
		H 1110	Indiv pers	
		H 1120	Families	
		H 1140	Places	H 910
–Literary style	x	H 1110	Indiv pers	
–Literary themes, motives	x	H 1160	Musical comps	
–Literature and the war, [revolution, etc.]	x	H 1200	Wars	
–Literatures	v	H 1140	Places	H 1828
–Liturgical lessons, Dutch, [English, etc.]	v	H 1188	Sacred works	
–Liturgical objects *(May Subd Geog)*	x	H 1185	Religions	
		H 1187	Christian denom	
–Liturgical use *(May Subd Geog)*	x	H 1188	Sacred works	
–Liturgy	x	H 1095	see *SCM:SH*	
		H 1186	Relig orders	
		H 1187	Christian denom	
–Liturgy–Calendar	x–v	H 1187	Christian denom	

SUBDIVISION	SUBFIELD CODE(S)	FREE-FLOATING LIST IN SCM:SH	CATEGORY	USAGE GUIDELINES IN SCM:SH
–Liturgy–Texts	x–v	H 1095 H 1186 H 1187	see *SCM:SH* Relig orders Christian denom	H 2190
–Liturgy–Texts–Concordances	x–x–v	H 1187	Christian denom	
–Liturgy–Texts–History and criticism	x–x–x	H 1187	Christian denom	
–Liturgy–Texts–Illustrations	x–x–v	H 1187	Christian denom	
–Liturgy–Texts–Manuscripts	x–v–v	H 1187	Christian denom	
–Liturgy–Texts–Rubrics	x–x–v	H 1187	Christian denom	
–Liturgy–Theology	x–x	H 1187	Christian denom	
–Liturgy, Experimental	x	H 1187	Christian denom	
–Location *(May Subd Geog)*	x	H 1095 H 1153 H 1180	see *SCM:SH* Industries Plants & crops	
–Locative constructions	x	H 1154	Languages	
–Locks	x	H 1195	Land vehicles	
–Locomotion *(May Subd Geog)*	x	H 1147	Animals	
–Logistics *(May Subd Geog)*	x	H 1200	Wars	
–Long-term care *(May Subd Geog)*	x	H 1100	Classes pers	
–Longevity *(May Subd Geog)*	x	H 1147 H 1180	Animals Plants & crops	
–Longitudinal studies	v	H 1095 H 1100 H 1103	see *SCM:SH* Classes pers Ethnic groups	H 1848 H 1848 H 1848
–Losses *(May Subd Geog)*	x	H 1147 H 1180	Animals Plants & crops	
–Losses–Prevention	x–x	H 1180	Plants & crops	
–Lubrication	x	H 1195	Land vehicles	
–Lutheran authors	x	H 1156	Literatures	

SUBDIVISION	SUBFIELD CODE(S)	FREE-FLOATING LIST IN SCM:SH	CATEGORY	USAGE GUIDELINES IN SCM:SH
–Luxembourg authors	x	H 1156	Literatures	
–Lymphatics	x	H 1164	Organs of body	
–Machinability	x	H 1158	Materials	
–Machine gun drill and tactics	x	H 1159	Military srvces	
–Machine translating *(May Subd Geog)*	x	H 1154	Languages	H 2219
–Machinery *(May Subd Geog)*	x	H 1180	Plants & crops	
–Magnetic fields	x	H 1164	Organs of body	
–Magnetic properties *(May Subd Geog)*	x	H 1149 H 1158	Chemicals Materials	
–Magnetic resonance imaging *(May Subd Geog)*	x	H 1150 H 1164	Diseases Organs of body	
–Maintenance and repair	x	H 1095 H 1195	see *SCM:SH* Land vehicles	
–Maintenance and repair–Law and legislation *(May Subd Geog)*	x–x	H 1195	Land vehicles	
–Majority leaders	x	H 1155	Legis bodies	
–Majority whips	x	H 1155	Legis bodies	
–Male authors	x	H 1156	Literatures	
–Management	x	H 1095 H 1105 H 1153 H 1159	see *SCM:SH* Corp bodies Industries Military srvces	
–Management–Employee participation *(May Subd Geog)*	x–x	H 1153	Industries	
–Management–Employee participation–Law and legislation *(May Subd Geog)*	x–x–x	H 1153	Industries	
–Maneuvers	x	H 1159	Military srvces	
–Manpower *(May Subd Geog)*	x	H 1200	Wars	

SUBDIVISION	SUBFIELD CODE(S)	FREE-FLOATING LIST IN SCM:SH	CATEGORY	USAGE GUIDELINES IN SCM:SH	
–Manure *(May Subd Geog)*	x	H 1147	Animals		
–Manure–Environmental aspects *(May Subd Geog)*	x–x	H 1147	Animals		
–Manure–Handling *(May Subd Geog)*	x–x	H 1147	Animals		
–Manuscripts	x	H 1095	see *SCM:SH*	H 1855	
		H 1100	Classes pers	H 1855	
		H 1103	Ethnic groups	H 1855	
		H 1110	Indiv pers	H 1855	
		H 1120	Families	H 1855	
		H 1156	Literatures	H 1855	
		H 1188	Sacred works	H 1855	
–Manuscripts–Catalogs	x–v	H 1095	see *SCM:SH*	H 1855	
–Manuscripts–Facsimiles	v–v	H 1095	see *SCM:SH*	H 1595	H 1855
		H 1110	Indiv pers	H 1595	H 1855
		H 1155.8	Lit works/Title	H 1595	H 1855
–Manuscripts–Indexes	x–v	H 1095	see *SCM:SH*		
–Manuscripts–Microform catalogs	x–v	H 1095	see *SCM:SH*	H 1361	
–Manuscripts–Paragraphs	x–x	H 1188	Sacred works		
–Manuscripts (Papyri)	x	H 1188	Sacred works		
–Manuscripts, English, [Latin, Aramaic, etc.]	x	H 1188	Sacred works	H 1855	
–Maori authors	x	H 1156	Literatures		
–Map collections	x	H 1105	Corp bodies	H 1427	
		H 1110	Indiv pers	H 1427	
		H 1120	Families	H 1427	
–Maps	v	H 1095	see *SCM:SH*		
		H 1103	Ethnic groups		
		H 1105	Corp bodies		
		H 1140	Places		
–Maps–Bibliography	x–v	H 1095	see *SCM:SH*		
		H 1105	Corp bodies		
		H 1140	Places		

SUBDIVISION	SUBFIELD CODE(S)	FREE-FLOATING LIST IN SCM:SH	CATEGORY	USAGE GUIDELINES IN SCM:SH
–Maps–Early works to 1800	v–v	H 1095 H 1140	see *SCM:SH* Places	
–Maps–Facsimiles	v–v	H 1095 H 1140	see *SCM:SH* Places	
–Maps–Symbols	x–x	H 1095	see *SCM:SH*	
–Maps, Comparative	v	H 1095 H 1140	see *SCM:SH* Places	
–Maps, Manuscript	v	H 1095 H 1140	see *SCM:SH* Places	
–Maps, Mental	v	H 1095 H 1140	see *SCM:SH* Places	
–Maps, Outline and base	v	H 1095 H 1140	see *SCM:SH* Places	
–Maps, Physical	v	H 1095 H 1140	see *SCM:SH* Places	
–Maps, Pictorial	v	H 1095 H 1140	see *SCM:SH* Places	
–Maps, Topographic	v	H 1095 H 1140	see *SCM:SH* Places	
–Maps, Tourist	v	H 1095 H 1140	see *SCM:SH* Places	
–Maps for children	v	H 1095 H 1105 H 1140	see *SCM:SH* Corp bodies Places	
–Maps for people with visual disabilities	v	H 1095 H 1140	see *SCM:SH* Places	
–Maps for the blind	v	H 1095 H 1140	see *SCM:SH* Places	
–Maratha authors	x	H 1156	Literatures	
–Marginal readings	v	H 1188	Sacred works	
–Markedness	x	H 1154	Languages	

SUBDIVISION	SUBFIELD CODE(S)	FREE-FLOATING LIST IN SCM:SH	CATEGORY	USAGE GUIDELINES IN SCM:SH
–Marketing	x	H 1095	see *SCM:SH*	H 1870
		H 1147	Animals	H 1870
		H 1180	Plants & crops	H 1870
		H 1195	Land vehicles	H 1870
–Marketing–Law and legislation *(May Subd Geog)*	x–x	H 1147	Animals	
–Marking *(May Subd Geog)*	x	H 1147	Animals	
–Marriage	x	H 1110	Indiv pers	
–Marriage customs and rites *(May Subd Geog)*	x	H 1103	Ethnic groups	
–Mascots	x	H 1151	Indiv schools	
		H 1159	Military srvces	
–Mass media and the war, [revolution, etc.]	x	H 1200	Wars	
–Massage *(May Subd Geog)*	x	H 1164	Organs of body	
–Masters-at-arms	x	H 1159	Military srvces	
–Material culture *(May Subd Geog)*	x	H 1103	Ethnic groups	
–Materials *(May Subd Geog)*	x	H 1095	see *SCM:SH*	
		H 1195	Land vehicles	
–Materials–Dynamic testing *(May Subd Geog)*	x–x	H 1195	Land vehicles	
–Materials management *(May Subd Geog)*	x	H 1153	Industries	
–Mathematical models	x	H 1095	see *SCM:SH*	H 2040
–Mathematics	x	H 1095	see *SCM:SH*	
		H 1103	Ethnic groups	
–Measurement	x	H 1095	see *SCM:SH*	
–Mechanical properties	x	H 1158	Materials	
		H 1164	Organs of body	
		H 1180	Plants & crops	
–Mechanism of action	x	H 1149	Chemicals	

SUBDIVISION	SUBFIELD CODE(S)	FREE-FLOATING LIST IN SCM:SH	CATEGORY	USAGE GUIDELINES IN SCM:SH
–Medals	x	H 1105 H 1110	Corp bodies Indiv pers	
–Medals *(May Subd Geog)*	x	H 1095 H 1100 H 1103 H 1200	see *SCM:SH* Classes pers Ethnic groups Wars	
–Medals, badges, decorations, etc.	x	H 1159	Military srvces	
–Medical care *(May Subd Geog)*	x	H 1100 H 1103 H 1159 H 1200	Classes pers Ethnic groups Military srvces Wars	
–Medical care–Law and legislation	x–x	H 1159	Military srvces	
–Medical examinations *(May Subd Geog)*	x	H 1095 H 1100 H 1103 H 1159	see *SCM:SH* Classes pers Ethnic groups Military srvces	
–Medical personnel	x	H 1159	Military srvces	
–Medical personnel–Malpractice	x–x	H 1159	Military srvces	
–Medical supplies	x	H 1159	Military srvces	
–Medical technologists	x	H 1159	Military srvces	
–Medicine *(May Subd Geog)*	x	H 1103	Ethnic groups	
–Medieval influences	x	H 1156	Literatures	H 1675
–Meditations	v	H 1095 H 1110 H 1188	see *SCM:SH* Indiv pers Sacred works	
–Mediterranean influences	x	H 1156	Literatures	H 1675
–Meiji period, 1868-1912	y	H 1148	Japanese art	
–Membership	x	H 1095 H 1105 H 1187	see *SCM:SH* Corp bodies Christian denom	
–Memorizing	x	H 1156 H 1188	Literatures Sacred works	

SUBDIVISION	SUBFIELD CODE(S)	FREE-FLOATING LIST IN SCM:SH	CATEGORY	USAGE GUIDELINES IN SCM:SH
–Mennonite authors	x	H 1156	Literatures	
–Mental health	x	H 1110	Indiv pers	H 1890
–Mental health *(May Subd Geog)*	x	H 1100	Classes pers	H 1890
		H 1103	Ethnic groups	H 1890
–Mental health services *(May Subd Geog)*	x	H 1100	Classes pers	H 1890
		H 1103	Ethnic groups	H 1890
–Mercury content *(May Subd Geog)*	x	H 1147	Animals	
–Mergers *(May Subd Geog)*	x	H 1151.5	Types schools	
		H 1153	Industries	
–Messes	x	H 1159	Military srvces	
–Metabolic detoxification *(May Subd Geog)*	x	H 1149	Chemicals	
–Metabolism	x	H 1147	Animals	
		H 1149	Chemicals	
		H 1164	Organs of body	
		H 1180	Plants & crops	
–Metabolism–Age factors *(May Subd Geog)*	x–x	H 1149	Chemicals	
–Metabolism–Climatic factors *(May Subd Geog)*	x–x	H 1147	Animals	
–Metabolism–Disorders *(May Subd Geog)*	x–x	H 1149	Chemicals	
		H 1164	Organs of body	
–Metabolism–Endocrine aspects	x–x	H 1164	Organs of body	
–Metabolism–Genetic aspects	x–x	H 1149	Chemicals	
–Metabolism–Regulation	x–x	H 1149	Chemicals	
		H 1164	Organs of body	
–Metallography	x	H 1158	Materials	
–Metallurgy	x	H 1158	Materials	
–Metamorphosis *(May Subd Geog)*	x	H 1147	Animals	
–Metamorphosis–Endocrine aspects	x–x	H 1147	Animals	

SUBDIVISION	SUBFIELD CODE(S)	FREE-FLOATING LIST IN SCM:SH	CATEGORY	USAGE GUIDELINES IN SCM:SH
–Metamorphosis–Genetic aspects	x–x	H 1147	Animals	
–Metamorphosis–Molecular aspects	x–x	H 1147	Animals	
–Methodist authors	x	H 1156	Literatures	
–Methodology	x	H 1095	see *SCM:SH*	
–Methods	v	H 1161	Musical instrum	
–Methods–Group instruction	v–v	H 1161	Musical instrum	
–Methods–Juvenile	v–v	H 1161	Musical instrum	
–Methods–Self-instruction	v–v	H 1161	Musical instrum	
–Methods (Alternative rock)	v	H 1161	Musical instrum	
–Methods (Alternative rock)–Group instruction	v–v	H 1161	Musical instrum	
–Methods (Alternative rock)–Self-instruction	v–v	H 1161	Musical instrum	
–Methods (Big band)	v	H 1161	Musical instrum	
–Methods (Big band)–Group instruction	v–v	H 1161	Musical instrum	
–Methods (Big band)–Self-instruction	v–v	H 1161	Musical instrum	
–Methods (Bluegrass)	v	H 1161	Musical instrum	
–Methods (Bluegrass)–Group instruction	v–v	H 1161	Musical instrum	
–Methods (Bluegrass)–Self-instruction	v–v	H 1161	Musical instrum	
–Methods (Blues)	v	H 1161	Musical instrum	
–Methods (Blues)–Group instruction	v–v	H 1161	Musical instrum	
–Methods (Blues)–Self-instruction	v–v	H 1161	Musical instrum	

SUBDIVISION	SUBFIELD CODE(S)	FREE-FLOATING LIST IN SCM:SH	CATEGORY	USAGE GUIDELINES IN SCM:SH
–Methods (Blues-rock)	v	H 1161	Musical instrum	
–Methods (Blues-rock)–Group instruction	v–v	H 1161	Musical instrum	
–Methods (Blues-rock)–Self-instruction	v–v	H 1161	Musical instrum	
–Methods (Boogie woogie)	v	H 1161	Musical instrum	
–Methods (Boogie woogie)–Group instruction	v–v	H 1161	Musical instrum	
–Methods (Boogie woogie)–Self-instruction	v–v	H 1161	Musical instrum	
–Methods (Bop)	v	H 1161	Musical instrum	
–Methods (Bop)–Group instruction	v–v	H 1161	Musical instrum	
–Methods (Bop)–Self-instruction	v–v	H 1161	Musical instrum	
–Methods (Celtic)	v	H 1161	Musical instrum	
–Methods (Celtic)–Group instruction	v–v	H 1161	Musical instrum	
–Methods (Celtic)–Self-instruction	v–v	H 1161	Musical instrum	
–Methods (Country)	v	H 1161	Musical instrum	
–Methods (Country)–Group instruction	v–v	H 1161	Musical instrum	
–Methods (Country)–Self-instruction	v–v	H 1161	Musical instrum	
–Methods (Dixieland)	v	H 1161	Musical instrum	
–Methods (Dixieland)–Group instruction	v–v	H 1161	Musical instrum	
–Methods (Dixieland)–Self-instruction	v–v	H 1161	Musical instrum	
–Methods (Folk)	v	H 1161	Musical instrum	

SUBDIVISION	SUBFIELD CODE(S)	FREE-FLOATING LIST IN SCM:SH	CATEGORY	USAGE GUIDELINES IN SCM:SH
–Methods (Folk)–Group instruction	v–v	H 1161	Musical instrum	
–Methods (Folk)–Self-instruction	v–v	H 1161	Musical instrum	
–Methods (Funk)	v	H 1161	Musical instrum	
–Methods (Funk)–Group instruction	v–v	H 1161	Musical instrum	
–Methods (Funk)–Self-instruction	v–v	H 1161	Musical instrum	
–Methods (Gospel)	v	H 1161	Musical instrum	
–Methods (Gospel)–Group instruction	v–v	H 1161	Musical instrum	
–Methods (Gospel)–Self-instruction	v–v	H 1161	Musical instrum	
–Methods (Heavy metal)	v	H 1161	Musical instrum	
–Methods (Heavy metal)–Group instruction	v–v	H 1161	Musical instrum	
–Methods (Heavy metal)–Self-instruction	v–v	H 1161	Musical instrum	
–Methods (Honky-tonk)	v	H 1161	Musical instrum	
–Methods (Honky-tonk)–Group instruction	v–v	H 1161	Musical instrum	
–Methods (Honky-tonk)–Self-instruction	v–v	H 1161	Musical instrum	
–Methods (Jazz)	v	H 1161	Musical instrum	
–Methods (Jazz)–Group instruction	v–v	H 1161	Musical instrum	
–Methods (Jazz)–Self-instruction	v–v	H 1161	Musical instrum	
–Methods (Jazz-rock)	v	H 1161	Musical instrum	
–Methods (Jazz-rock)–Group instruction	v–v	H 1161	Musical instrum	
–Methods (Jazz-rock)–Self-instruction	v–v	H 1161	Musical instrum	

SUBDIVISION	SUBFIELD CODE(S)	FREE-FLOATING LIST IN SCM:SH	CATEGORY	USAGE GUIDELINES IN SCM:SH
–Methods (Latin jazz)	v	H 1161	Musical instrum	
–Methods (Latin jazz)–Group instruction	v–v	H 1161	Musical instrum	
–Methods (Latin jazz)–Self-instruction	v–v	H 1161	Musical instrum	
–Methods (Popular music)	v	H 1161	Musical instrum	
–Methods (Popular music)–Group instruction	v–v	H 1161	Musical instrum	
–Methods (Popular music)–Self-instruction	v–v	H 1161	Musical instrum	
–Methods (Progressive rock)	v	H 1161	Musical instrum	
–Methods (Progressive rock)–Group instruction	v–v	H 1161	Musical instrum	
–Methods (Progressive rock)–Self-instruction	v–v	H 1161	Musical instrum	
–Methods (Ragtime)	v	H 1161	Musical instrum	
–Methods (Ragtime)–Group instruction	v–v	H 1161	Musical instrum	
–Methods (Ragtime)–Self-instruction	v–v	H 1161	Musical instrum	
–Methods (Reggae)	v	H 1161	Musical instrum	
–Methods (Reggae)–Group instruction	v–v	H 1161	Musical instrum	
–Methods (Reggae)–Self-instruction	v–v	H 1161	Musical instrum	
–Methods (Rhythm and blues)	v	H 1161	Musical instrum	
–Methods (Rhythm and blues)–Group instruction	v–v	H 1161	Musical instrum	
–Methods (Rhythm and blues)–Self-instruction	v–v	H 1161	Musical instrum	

SUBDIVISION	SUBFIELD CODE(S)	FREE-FLOATING LIST IN SCM:SH	CATEGORY	USAGE GUIDELINES IN SCM:SH	
–Methods (Rock)	v	H 1161	Musical instrum		
–Methods (Rock)–Group instruction	v–v	H 1161	Musical instrum		
–Methods (Rock)–Self-instruction	v–v	H 1161	Musical instrum		
–Methods (Swing)	v	H 1161	Musical instrum		
–Methods (Swing)–Group instruction	v–v	H 1161	Musical instrum		
–Methods (Swing)–Self-instruction	v–v	H 1161	Musical instrum		
–Methods (Western swing)	v	H 1161	Musical instrum		
–Methods (Western swing)–Group instruction	v–v	H 1161	Musical instrum		
–Methods (Western swing)–Self-instruction	v–v	H 1161	Musical instrum		
–Methylation	x	H 1149	Chemicals		
–Metonyms	x	H 1154	Languages		
–Metrics and rhythmics	x	H 1154	Languages		
–Mexican Americans	x	H 1200	Wars		
–Mexican influences	x	H 1156	Literatures	H 1675	
–Microbiology (May Subd Geog)	x	H 1147	Animals		
		H 1150	Diseases		
		H 1158	Materials		
		H 1164	Organs of body		
		H 1180	Plants & crops		
–Microform catalogs	v	H 1095	see SCM:SH	H 1361	H 1965
		H 1105	Corp bodies	H 1361	H 1965
–Micropropagation (May Subd Geog)	x	H 1180	Plants & crops		
–Microscopy (May Subd Geog)	x	H 1158	Materials		
		H 1164	Organs of body		
		H 1180	Plants & crops		
–Microstructure	x	H 1158	Materials		

SUBDIVISION	SUBFIELD CODE(S)	FREE-FLOATING LIST IN SCM:SH	CATEGORY	USAGE GUIDELINES IN SCM:SH
–Middle English, 1100-1500	y	H 1154 H 1155.2 H 1156	Languages Groups lit auth Literatures	
–Migration *(May Subd Geog)*	x	H 1147	Animals	
–Migration–Climatic factors *(May Subd Geog)*	x–x	H 1147	Animals	
–Migration–Endocrine aspects	x	H 1147	Animals	
–Migrations	x	H 1103	Ethnic groups	
–Military aspects *(May Subd Geog)*	x	H 1153	Industries	
–Military capital	x	H 1159	Military srvces	
–Military construction operations	x	H 1159	Military srvces	
–Military construction operations–Law and legislation	x–x	H 1159	Military srvces	
–Military currency *(May Subd Geog)*	x	H 1200	Wars	
–Military intelligence *(May Subd Geog)*	x	H 1200	Wars	
–Military leadership	x	H 1110	Indiv pers	
–Military life	x	H 1159	Military srvces	
–Military police	x	H 1159	Military srvces	
–Military police–Foreign auxiliaries	x–x	H 1159	Military srvces	
–Military policy	x	H 1140	Places	
–Military policy–Religious aspects	x–x	H 1140	Places	
–Military relations *(May Subd Geog)*	x	H 1140	Places	H 1996
–Military relations–Foreign countries	x–z	H 1140	Places	
–Militia	x	H 1140	Places	
–Milling *(May Subd Geog)*	x	H 1180	Plants & crops	

SUBDIVISION	SUBFIELD CODE(S)	FREE-FLOATING LIST IN SCM:SH	CATEGORY	USAGE GUIDELINES IN SCM:SH
–Mimetic words	x	H 1154	Languages	
–Minangkabau influences	x	H 1156	Literatures	H 1675
–Ming-Qing dynasties, 1368-1912	y	H 1148	Chinese art	
–Minorities	x	H 1159	Military srvces	
–Minority authors	x	H 1156	Literatures	
–Minority leaders	x	H 1155	Legis bodies	
–Minority whips	x	H 1155	Legis bodies	
–Miracles	x	H 1110	Indiv pers	
–Miscellanea	v	H 1095	see *SCM:SH*	H 1910
–Misfueling *(May Subd Geog)*	x	H 1195	Land vehicles	
–Missing in action *(May Subd Geog)*	x	H 1200	Wars	
–Missions *(May Subd Geog)*	x	H 1103	Ethnic groups	
		H 1185	Religions	
		H 1186	Relig orders	
		H 1187	Christian denom	
–Mixing *(May Subd Geog)*	x	H 1158	Materials	
–Mnemonic devices	x	H 1188	Sacred works	
–Mobilization	x	H 1159	Military srvces	
–Modality	x	H 1154	Languages	
–Models *(May Subd Geog)*	x	H 1095	see *SCM:SH*	H 2040
		H 1164	Organs of body	
		H 1195	Land vehicles	
–Models–Finishing *(May Subd Geog)*	x–x	H 1195	Land vehicles	
–Models–Radio control *(May Subd Geog)*	x–x	H 1195	Land vehicles	
–Moisture *(May Subd Geog)*	x	H 1095	see *SCM:SH*	
		H 1158	Materials	
		H 1180	Plants & crops	

SUBDIVISION	SUBFIELD CODE(S)	FREE-FLOATING LIST IN SCM:SH	CATEGORY	USAGE GUIDELINES IN SCM:SH
–Molecular aspects	x	H 1147	Animals	
		H 1150	Diseases	
		H 1164	Organs of body	
		H 1180	Plants & crops	
–Molecular diagnosis *(May Subd Geog)*	x	H 1150	Diseases	
–Molecular genetics	x	H 1147	Animals	
		H 1180	Plants & crops	
–Molecular rotation	x	H 1149	Chemicals	
–Money *(May Subd Geog)*	x	H 1103	Ethnic groups	
–Mongolian authors	x	H 1156	Literatures	
–Monitoring *(May Subd Geog)*	x	H 1147	Animals	
		H 1180	Plants & crops	
–Monosyllables	x	H 1154	Languages	
–Monuments *(May Subd Geog)*	x	H 1100	Classes pers	
		H 1103	Ethnic groups	
		H 1110	Indiv pers	H 1334
		H 1120	Families	
		H 1200	Wars	
–Mood	x	H 1154	Languages	
–Moral and ethical aspects *(May Subd Geog)*	x	H 1095	see *SCM:SH*	H 1998
		H 1200	Wars	H 1998
–Moral conditions	x	H 1140	Places	
–Mormon authors	x	H 1156	Literatures	
–Morphemics	x	H 1154	Languages	
–Morphogenesis *(May Subd Geog)*	x	H 1147	Animals	
		H 1180	Plants & crops	
–Morphology	x	H 1147	Animals	
		H 1154	Languages	
		H 1180	Plants & crops	
–Morphophonemics	x	H 1154	Languages	

SUBDIVISION	SUBFIELD CODE(S)	FREE-FLOATING LIST IN SCM:SH	CATEGORY	USAGE GUIDELINES IN SCM:SH
–Morphosyntax	x	H 1154	Languages	
–Mortality *(May Subd Geog)*	x	H 1100	Classes pers	
		H 1103	Ethnic groups	
		H 1147	Animals	
		H 1150	Diseases	
–Motion picture plays	x	H 1110	Indiv pers	
–Motion pictures and the war, [revolution, etc.]	x	H 1200	Wars	
–Motorcycle troops	x	H 1159	Military srvces	
–Motors	x	H 1195	Land vehicles	
–Motors–Bearings *(May Subd Geog)*	x–x	H 1195	Land vehicles	
–Motors–Camshafts	x–x	H 1195	Land vehicles	
–Motors–Carburetors	x–x	H 1195	Land vehicles	
–Motors–Combustion *(May Subd Geog)*	x	H 1195	Land vehicles	
–Motors–Computer control systems *(May Subd Geog)*	x–x	H 1195	Land vehicles	
–Motors–Control systems	x–x	H 1195	Land vehicles	
–Motors–Cooling *(May Subd Geog)*	x–x	H 1195	Land vehicles	
–Motors–Cooling systems *(May Subd Geog)*	x–x	H 1195	Land vehicles	
–Motors–Crankshafts	x–x	H 1195	Land vehicles	
–Motors–Cylinder blocks	x–x	H 1195	Land vehicles	
–Motors–Cylinder heads *(May Subd Geog)*	x–x	H 1195	Land vehicles	
–Motors–Cylinders	x–x	H 1195	Land vehicles	
–Motors–Electronic fuel injection systems	x–x	H 1195	Land vehicles	

SUBDIVISION	SUBFIELD CODE(S)	FREE-FLOATING LIST IN SCM:SH	CATEGORY	USAGE GUIDELINES IN SCM:SH
–Motors–Exhaust gas *(May Subd Geog)*	x–x	H 1195	Land vehicles	
–Motors–Exhaust gas–Law and legislation *(May Subd Geog)*	x–x–x	H 1195	Land vehicles	
–Motors–Exhaust systems	x–x	H 1195	Land vehicles	
–Motors–Fuel injection systems	x–x	H 1195	Land vehicles	
–Motors–Knock *(May Subd Geog)*	x–x	H 1195	Land vehicles	
–Motors–Lubrication systems *(May Subd Geog)*	x–x	H 1195	Land vehicles	
–Motors–Modification *(May Subd Geog)*	x–x	H 1195	Land vehicles	
–Motors–Mufflers	x–x	H 1195	Land vehicles	
–Motors–Mufflers–Acoustic properties *(May Subd Geog)*	x–x–x	H 1195	Land vehicles	
–Motors–Oil filters	x–x	H 1195	Land vehicles	
–Motors–Parts *(May Subd Geog)*	x–x	H 1195	Land vehicles	
–Motors–Pistons and piston rings	x–x	H 1195	Land vehicles	
–Motors–Soundproofing *(May Subd Geog)*	x–x	H 1195	Land vehicles	
–Motors–Superchargers	x–x	H 1195	Land vehicles	
–Motors–Timing belts	x–x	H 1195	Land vehicles	
–Motors–Turbochargers	x–x	H 1195	Land vehicles	
–Motors–Valves *(May Subd Geog)*	x–x	H 1195	Land vehicles	
–Motors–Vibration *(May Subd Geog)*	x–x	H 1195	Land vehicles	
–Motors (Compressed-gas) *(May Subd Geog)*	x	H 1195	Land vehicles	
–Motors (Diesel)	x	H 1195	Land vehicles	

SUBDIVISION	SUBFIELD CODE(S)	FREE-FLOATING LIST IN SCM:SH	CATEGORY	USAGE GUIDELINES IN SCM:SH
–Motors (Diesel)–Exhaust gas *(May Subd Geog)*	x	H 1195	Land vehicles	
–Motors (Liquid nitrogen) *(May Subd Geog)*	x	H 1195	Land vehicles	
–Motors (Two-stroke cycle)	x	H 1195	Land vehicles	
–Movements	x	H 1164	Organs of body	
–Mulching *(May Subd Geog)*	x	H 1180	Plants	
–Multiphonics	x	H 1161	Musical instrum	
–Muscles	x	H 1164	Organs of body	
–Museums	x	H 1105	Corp bodies	H 1916
–Museums *(May Subd Geog)*	x	H 1095	see *SCM:SH*	H 1916
		H 1100	Classes pers	H 1916
		H 1103	Ethnic groups	H 1916
		H 1110	Indiv pers	H 1916
		H 1120	Families	H 1916
		H 1187	Christian denom	H 1916
		H 1200	Wars	H 1916
–Music	v	H 1103	Ethnic groups	H 1917
–Music–Bibliography	x–v	H 1103	Ethnic groups	
–Music–Discography	x–v	H 1103	Ethnic groups	
–Music–History and criticism	x–x	H 1103	Ethnic groups	
–Music and the war, [revolution, etc.]	x	H 1200	Wars	
–Musical instrument collections	x	H 1105	Corp bodies	H 1427
		H 1110	Indiv pers	H 1427
		H 1120	Families	H 1427
–Musical settings	v	H 1110	Indiv pers	
		H 1156	Literatures	
–Musical settings–History and criticism	x–x	H 1110	Indiv pers	
		H 1156	Literatures	
–Muslim authors	x	H 1156	Literatures	

Free-floating Subdivisions: An Alphabetical Index

SUBDIVISION	SUBFIELD CODE(S)	FREE-FLOATING LIST IN SCM:SH	CATEGORY	USAGE GUIDELINES IN SCM:SH
–Mutation	x	H 1154	Languages	
–Mutation breeding *(May Subd Geog)*	x	H 1180	Plants & crops	
–Mutual intelligibility	x	H 1154	Languages	
–Mycenaean influences	x	H 1156	Literatures	H 1675
–Mythology *(May Subd Geog)*	x	H 1095	see *SCM:SH*	H 1998
–Name	x	H 1095	see *SCM:SH*	H 1919
		H 1103	Ethnic groups	H 1919
		H 1105	Corp bodies	H 1919
		H 1110	Indiv pers	H 1919
		H 1140	Places	H 1919
		H 1187	Christian denom	H 1919
		H 1200	Wars	H 1919
–Names	x	H 1095	see *SCM:SH*	H 1919
		H 1147	Animals	H 1919
		H 1151.5	Types schools	H 1919
–Nasality	x	H 1154	Languages	
–National Guard	x	H 1140	Places	
–Natural history collections	x	H 1105	Corp bodies	H 1427
		H 1110	Indiv pers	H 1427
		H 1120	Families	H 1427
–Naval militia	x	H 1140	Places	
–Naval operations	x	H 1200	Wars	
–Naval operations–Submarine	x–x	H 1200	Wars	
–Naval operations, American, [British, etc.]	x	H 1200	Wars	
–Navigation	x	H 1145.5	Bodies water	
–Navigation–Law and legislation	x–x	H 1145.5	Bodies water	
–Nazi persecution *(May Subd Geog)*	x	H 1186	Relig orders	
–Necrology	v	H 1186	Relig orders	

SUBDIVISION	SUBFIELD CODE(S)	FREE-FLOATING LIST IN SCM:SH	CATEGORY	USAGE GUIDELINES IN SCM:SH
–Necrosis *(May Subd Geog)*	x	H 1164	Organs of body	
–Needle biopsy *(May Subd Geog)*	x	H 1164	Organs of body	
–Negatives	x	H 1154	Languages	
–Nervous system	x	H 1147	Animals	
–Nests *(May Subd Geog)*	x	H 1147	Animals	
–Nests–Abandonment *(May Subd Geog)*	x–x	H 1147	Animals	
–Nests–Counting *(May Subd Geog)*	x–x	H 1147	Animals	
–Neutralization	x	H 1154	Languages	
–New words	x	H 1154	Languages	
–Newspapers	v	H 1095	see *SCM:SH*	H 1920
		H 1103	Ethnic groups	H 1920
		H 1140	Places	
–Nitrogen content *(May Subd Geog)*	x	H 1158	Materials	
–Noise	x	H 1095	see *SCM:SH*	
		H 1153	Industries	
–Nomenclature	v	H 1095	see *SCM:SH*	
		H 1147	Animals	
		H 1180	Plants & crops	
–Nomenclature (Popular)	v	H 1147	Animals	
		H 1180	Plants & crops	
–Nomenclature (Popular)–French, [Italian, etc.]	v–x	H 1147	Animals	
–Nominals	x	H 1154	Languages	
–Nomograms	v	H 1095	see *SCM:SH*	
–Non-commissioned officers	x	H 1159	Military srvces	
–Non-commissioned officers' handbooks	v	H 1159	Military srvces	

SUBDIVISION	SUBFIELD CODE(S)	FREE-FLOATING LIST IN SCM:SH	CATEGORY	USAGE GUIDELINES IN SCM:SH
–Nondestructive testing *(May Subd Geog)*	x	H 1158	Materials	
–Notation	v	H 1095	see *SCM:SH*	
–Notebooks, sketchbooks, etc.	v	H 1110	Indiv pers	
–Noun	x	H 1154	Languages	
–Noun phrase	x	H 1154	Languages	
–Number	x	H 1154	Languages	
–Numerals	x	H 1154	Languages	
–Numerical division	x	H 1188	Sacred works	
–Numismatic collections	x	H 1105	Corp bodies	H 1427
		H 1110	Indiv pers	H 1427
		H 1120	Families	H 1427
–Numismatics	x	H 1110	Indiv pers	
–Nurses	x	H 1159	Military srvces	
–Nursing *(May Subd Geog)*	x	H 1150	Diseases	
–Nursing home care *(May Subd Geog)*	x	H 1100	Classes pers	
–Nutrition *(May Subd Geog)*	x	H 1100	Classes pers	
		H 1103	Ethnic groups	
		H 1147	Animals	
		H 1180	Plants & crops	
–Nutrition–Requirements *(May Subd Geog)*	x–x	H 1100	Classes pers	
		H 1147	Animals	
–Nutritional aspects *(May Subd Geog)*	x	H 1150	Diseases	
–Obituaries	v	H 1100	Classes pers	
		H 1103	Ethnic groups	
–Obscene words	x	H 1154	Languages	
–Observations	v	H 1095	see *SCM:SH*	

SUBDIVISION	SUBFIELD CODE(S)	FREE-FLOATING LIST IN SCM:SH	CATEGORY	USAGE GUIDELINES IN SCM:SH
–Observers' manuals	v	H 1095	see *SCM:SH*	H 1646
–Obsolete words	x	H 1154	Languages	
–Occupant restraint systems (*May Subd Geog*)	x	H 1195	Land vehicles	
–Occupational specialties	x	H 1159	Military srvces	
–Occupations	x	H 1186	Relig orders	
–Occupied territories	x	H 1200	Wars	
–Odor (*May Subd Geog*)	x	H 1147	Animals	
–Off-road operation (*May Subd Geog*)	x	H 1195	Land vehicles	
–Officer efficiency reports	x	H 1159	Military srvces	
–Officers	x	H 1159	Military srvces	
–Officers' clubs	x	H 1159	Military srvces	
–Officers' handbooks	v	H 1159	Military srvces	
–Officers on detached service	x	H 1159	Military srvces	
–Officials and employees	x	H 1095	see *SCM:SH*	
		H 1105	Corp bodies	
		H 1149.5	Colonies	
		H 1155	Legis bodies	
		H 1159	Military srvces	
–Officials and employees (*May Subd Geog*)	x	H 1140	Places	
–Officials and employees–Accidents (*May Subd Geog*)	x–x	H 1105	Corp bodies	
		H 1140	Places	
–Officials and employees–Foreign countries	x–z	H 1140	Places	
–Officials and employees–Foreign countries–Foreign language competency	x–z–x	H 1140	Places	

SUBDIVISION	SUBFIELD CODE(S)	FREE-FLOATING LIST IN SCM:SH	CATEGORY	USAGE GUIDELINES IN SCM:SH
–Officials and employees–Furloughs	x–x	H 1105 H 1140	Corp bodies Places	
–Officials and employees–Leave regulations	x–x	H 1105 H 1140	Corp bodies Places	
–Officials and employees–Payroll deductions	x–x	H 1140	Places	
–Officials and employees–Pensions	x–x	H 1155	Legis bodies	
–Officials and employees–Salaries, etc.	x–x	H 1105 H 1155	Corp bodies Legis bodies	
–Officials and employees–Salaries, etc. *(May Subd Geog)*	x–x	H 1140	Places	
–Officials and employees–Salaries, etc.–Regional disparities	x–x–x	H 1105 H 1140	Corp bodies Places	
–Officials and employees–Turnover	x–x	H 1105 H 1140	Corp bodies Places	
–Officials and employees, Alien	x	H 1140	Places	
–Officials and employees, Honorary	x	H 1140	Places	
–Officials and employees, Retired	x	H 1140	Places	
–Old English, ca. 450-1100	y	H 1154 H 1155.2 H 1156	Languages Groups lit auth Literatures	
–Old Norse influences	x	H 1156	Literatures	H 1675
–On postage stamps	x	H 1105 H 1110 H 1140 H 1187	Corp bodies Indiv pers Places Christian denom	H 1945 H 1945 H 1945 H 1945
–On television	x	H 1110 H 1140	Indiv pers Places	
–Online chat groups	v	H 1095	see *SCM:SH*	
–Onomatopoeic words	x	H 1154	Languages	
–Open admission	x	H 1151	Indiv schools	

SUBDIVISION	SUBFIELD CODE(S)	FREE-FLOATING LIST IN SCM:SH	CATEGORY	USAGE GUIDELINES IN SCM:SH
–Open admission *(May Subd Geog)*	x	H 1151.5	Types schools	
–Operational readiness	x	H 1159	Military srvces	
–Operations other than war	x	H 1159	Military srvces	
–Optical instrument repairers	x	H 1159	Military srvces	
–Optical properties	x	H 1149 H 1158	Chemicals Materials	
–Oratory	x	H 1110	Indiv pers	
–Orbit	x	H 1095	see *SCM:SH*	
–Orchestral excerpts	v	H 1161	Musical instrum	
–Orchestras	x	H 1151	Indiv schools	
–Order-books	v	H 1159	Military srvces	
–Ordnance and ordnance stores	x	H 1159	Military srvces	
–Ordnance and ordnance stores– Effect of environment on *(May Subd Geog)*	x	H 1159	Military srvces	H 1580
–Ordnance and ordnance stores– Quality control	x	H 1159	Military srvces	
–Ordnance facilities	x	H 1159	Military srvces	
–Organ scores	v	H 1160	Musical comps	
–Organization	x	H 1159	Military srvces	
–Organs	x	H 1105	Corp bodies	
–Orientation *(May Subd Geog)*	x	H 1147	Animals	
–Origin	x	H 1103 H 1147 H 1180 H 1185	Ethnic groups Animals Plants & crops Religions	
–Orthodox Eastern authors	x	H 1156	Literatures	
–Orthography and spelling	x	H 1154	Languages	

SUBDIVISION	SUBFIELD CODE(S)	FREE-FLOATING LIST IN SCM:SH	CATEGORY	USAGE GUIDELINES IN SCM:SH
–Osmotic potential *(May Subd Geog)*	x	H 1180	Plants & crops	
–Outlines, syllabi, etc.	v	H 1095	see *SCM:SH*	
		H 1100	Classes pers	
		H 1103	Ethnic groups	
		H 1110	Indiv pers	
		H 1188	Sacred works	
–Overdose *(May Subd Geog)*	x	H 1149	Chemicals	
–Ownership *(May Subd Geog)*	x	H 1153	Industries	
–Oxidation *(May Subd Geog)*	x	H 1149	Chemicals	
–Oxygen content *(May Subd Geog)*	x	H 1158	Materials	
–Packaging *(May Subd Geog)*	x	H 1095	see *SCM:SH*	
		H 1180	Plants & crops	
–Packing *(May Subd Geog)*	x	H 1095	see *SCM:SH*	
		H 1180	Plants & crops	
–Painting *(May Subd Geog)*	x	H 1158	Materials	
		H 1195	Land vehicles	
–Painting of vessels	x	H 1159	Military srvces	
–Palaces *(May Subd Geog)*	x	H 1110	Indiv pers	
–Palatalization	x	H 1154	Languages	
–Palliative treatment *(May Subd Geog)*	x	H 1150	Diseases	
–Palynotaxonomy *(May Subd Geog)*	x	H 1180	Plants & crops	
–Pamphlets	v	H 1095	see *SCM:SH*	
		H 1200	Wars	
–Papal documents	v	H 1095	see *SCM:SH*	
–Parables	x	H 1188	Sacred works	
–Parachute troops	x	H 1159	Military srvces	
–Paragraphs	x	H 1154	Languages	
		H 1188	Sacred works	

SUBDIVISION	SUBFIELD CODE(S)	FREE-FLOATING LIST IN SCM:SH	CATEGORY	USAGE GUIDELINES IN SCM:SH
–Parallel versions, English, [French, etc.]	v	H 1188	Sacred works	
–Parallelism	x	H 1154	Languages	
–Paralysis *(May Subd Geog)*	x	H 1164	Organs of body	
–Paraphrase	x	H 1154	Languages	
–Paraphrases	v	H 1188	Sacred works	
–Paraphrases–History and criticism	x–x	H 1188	Sacred works	
–Paraphrases, English, [French, German, etc.]	v	H 1188	Sacred works	
–Paraphrases, English, [French, German, etc.]–History and criticism	x–x	H 1188	Sacred works	
–Parasites *(May Subd Geog)*	x	H 1147 H 1164	Animals Organs of body	
–Parasites–Biological control *(May Subd Geog)*	x–x	H 1147	Animals	
–Parasites–Control *(May Subd Geog)*	x–x	H 1147	Animals	
–Parasites–Control–Environmental aspects *(May Subd Geog)*	x–x–x	H 1147	Animals	
–Parasites–Identification	x–v	H 1147	Animals	
–Parasites–Life cycles *(May Subd Geog)*	x–x	H 1147	Animals	
–Parasites–Molecular aspects	x–x	H 1147	Animals	
–Pardon	x	H 1110	Indiv pers	
–Parenthetical constructions	x	H 1154	Languages	
–Parking	x	H 1151	Indiv schools	

SUBDIVISION	SUBFIELD CODE(S)	FREE-FLOATING LIST IN SCM:SH	CATEGORY	USAGE GUIDELINES IN SCM:SH
–Parodies, imitations, etc.	v	H 1095 H 1110 H 1155.8 H 1188	see *SCM:SH* Indiv pers Lit works/Title Sacred works	
–Paronyms	x	H 1154	Languages	
–Parsee authors	x	H 1156	Literatures	
–Parsing	x	H 1154	Languages	
–Participation, African American, [Indian, etc.]	x	H 1200	Wars	
–Participation, Buddhist, [Muslim, etc.]	x	H 1200	Wars	
–Participation, Communist	x	H 1200	Wars	
–Participation, Female	x	H 1200	Wars	
–Participation, Foreign	x	H 1200	Wars	
–Participation, Gay	x	H 1200	Wars	
–Participation, German, [Irish, Swiss, etc.]	x	H 1200	Wars	
–Participation, Immigrant	x	H 1200	Wars	
–Participation, Jewish	x	H 1200	Wars	
–Participation, Juvenile	x	H 1200	Wars	
–Participle	x	H 1154	Languages	
–Particles	x	H 1154	Languages	
–Partitives	x	H 1154	Languages	
–Parts	v	H 1160	Musical comps	
–Parts *(May Subd Geog)*	x	H 1195	Land vehicles	
–Parts–Law and legislation *(May Subd Geog)*	x–x	H 1195	Land vehicles	
–Parts (solo)	v	H 1160	Musical comps	

SUBDIVISION	SUBFIELD CODE(S)	FREE-FLOATING LIST IN SCM:SH	CATEGORY	USAGE GUIDELINES IN SCM:SH
–Parts of speech	x	H 1154	Languages	
–Parturition (May Subd Geog)	x	H 1147	Animals	
–Party work	x	H 1105	Corp bodies	
–Passenger lists	v	H 1095	see SCM:SH	
–Passive voice	x	H 1154	Languages	
–Pastoral counseling of (May Subd Geog)	x	H 1100 H 1103	Classes pers Ethnic groups	
–Pastoral letters and charges	v	H 1187	Christian denom	
–Patents	v	H 1095	see SCM:SH	
–Pathogenesis	x	H 1150	Diseases	
–Pathogens (May Subd Geog)	x	H 1147	Animals	
–Pathophysiology	x	H 1149 H 1150 H 1164	Chemicals Diseases Organs of body	
–Pathophysiology–Animal models	x–x	H 1164	Organs of body	
–Patients (May Subd Geog)	x	H 1150	Diseases	
–Pay, allowances, etc.	x	H 1159	Military srvces	
–Pay, allowances, etc.–Law and legislation	x–x	H 1159	Military srvces	
–Peace	x	H 1200	Wars	
–Pedaling	x	H 1161	Musical instrum	
–Pedigrees	v	H 1147	Animals	
–Pejoration	x	H 1154	Languages	
–Penetration resistance	x	H 1158	Materials	
–Pensions	x	H 1155	Legis bodies	
–Pensions (May Subd Geog)	x	H 1100 H 1103	Classes pers Ethnic groups	

SUBDIVISION	SUBFIELD CODE(S)	FREE-FLOATING LIST IN SCM:SH	CATEGORY	USAGE GUIDELINES IN SCM:SH
–Pensions–Cost-of-living adjustments *(May Subd Geog)*	x–x	H 1100	Classes pers	
–Pensions–Effect of inflation on *(May Subd Geog)*	x–x	H 1100	Classes pers	
–Pensions–Unclaimed benefits *(May Subd Geog)*	x–x	H 1100	Classes pers	
–Performance *(May Subd Geog)*	x	H 1161 H 1195	Musical instrum Land vehicles	
–Performance records	v	H 1147	Animals	
–Performances *(May Subd Geog)*	x	H 1105 H 1110 H 1160	Corp bodies Indiv pers Musical comps	
–Periodicals	v	H 1095	see *SCM:SH*	H 1927
–Periodicals–Abbreviations of titles	x–v	H 1095	see *SCM:SH*	
–Periodicals–Bibliography	x–v	H 1095	see *SCM:SH*	
–Periodicals–Bibliography–Catalogs	x–v–v	H 1095	see *SCM:SH*	H 1361
–Periodicals–Bibliography–Union lists	x–v–v	H 1095	see *SCM:SH*	H 1361
–Periodicals–Indexes	x–v	H 1095	see *SCM:SH*	H 1670
–Periodization	x	H 1156	Literatures	
–Permeability	x	H 1149 H 1158 H 1164	Chemicals Materials Organs of body	
–Peroxidation	x	H 1149	Chemicals	
–Persian authors	x	H 1156	Literatures	
–Persian influences	x	H 1156	Literatures	H 1675
–Person	x	H 1154	Languages	

SUBDIVISION	SUBFIELD CODE(S)	FREE-FLOATING LIST IN SCM:SH	CATEGORY	USAGE GUIDELINES IN SCM:SH
–Personal narratives	v	H 1095	see *SCM:SH*	H 1928
		H 1200	Wars	H 1928
–Personal narratives, American, [French, etc.]	v	H 1200	Wars	H 1928
–Personal narratives, Confederate	v	H 1200	Wars	H 1928
–Personal narratives, Jewish	v	H 1200	Wars	H 1928
–Personnel management	x	H 1095	see *SCM:SH*	
		H 1105	Corp bodies	
		H 1153	Industries	
		H 1159	Military srvces	
–Personnel management–Law and legislation	x–x	H 1159	Military srvces	
–Personnel records	x	H 1105	Corp bodies	
		H 1159	Military srvces	
–Petty officers	x	H 1159	Military srvces	
–Petty officers' handbooks	v	H 1159	Military srvces	
–Pharmacokinetics	x	H 1149	Chemicals	
–Phenology	x	H 1180	Plants & crops	
–Philosophy	x	H 1095	see *SCM:SH*	H 1929
		H 1110	Indiv pers	H 1929
		H 1155.2	Groups lit auth	H 1929
		H 1188	Sacred works	H 1929
–Phonemics	x	H 1154	Languages	
–Phonetic transcriptions	v	H 1154	Languages	
–Phonetics	x	H 1154	Languages	
–Phonology	x	H 1154	Languages	
–Phonology, Comparative	x	H 1154	Languages	
–Phonology, Comparative–French, [German, etc.]	x–x	H 1154	Languages	
–Phonology, Historical	x	H 1154	Languages	

SUBDIVISION	SUBFIELD CODE(S)	FREE-FLOATING LIST IN SCM:SH	CATEGORY	USAGE GUIDELINES IN SCM:SH
–Photochemotherapy *(May Subd Geog)*	x	H 1150	Diseases	
–Photograph collections	x	H 1105 H 1110 H 1120	Corp bodies Indiv pers Families	
–Photographers	x	H 1159	Military srvces	
–Photographic identification *(May Subd Geog)*	x	H 1147	Animals	
–Photographs	v	H 1095	see *SCM:SH*	H 1935
–Photographs from space	v	H 1095 H 1140	see *SCM:SH* Places	
–Photography	x	H 1200	Wars	
–Photomorphogenesis	x	H 1180	Plants & crops	
–Phototherapy *(May Subd Geog)*	x	H 1150	Diseases	
–Phraseology	x	H 1154	Languages	
–Phylogeny	x	H 1147 H 1164 H 1180	Animals Organs of body Plants & crops	
–Phylogeny–Molecular aspects	x	H 1147 H 1180	Animals Plants & crops	
–Physical therapy *(May Subd Geog)*	x	H 1150	Diseases	
–Physical training *(May Subd Geog)*	x	H 1159	Military srvces	
–Physiological aspects	x	H 1095	see *SCM:SH*	
–Physiological effect *(May Subd Geog)*	x	H 1095 H 1149 H 1158 H 1180	see *SCM:SH* Chemicals Materials Plants & crops	
–Physiological genomics	x	H 1147	Animals	
–Physiological transport	x	H 1149	Chemicals	

SUBDIVISION	SUBFIELD CODE(S)	FREE-FLOATING LIST IN SCM:SH	CATEGORY	USAGE GUIDELINES IN SCM:SH
–Physiology *(May Subd Geog)*	x	H 1100	Classes pers	
		H 1103	Ethnic groups	
		H 1147	Animals	
		H 1164	Organs of body	
		H 1180	Plants & crops	
–Piano scores	v	H 1160	Musical comps	
–Piano scores (4 hands)	v	H 1160	Musical comps	
–Pickling *(May Subd Geog)*	x	H 1158	Materials	
–Pickling–By-products	x–x	H 1158	Materials	
–Pickling–Waste disposal *(May Subd Geog)*	x–x	H 1158	Materials	
–Pictorial works	v	H 1095	see *SCM:SH*	H 1935
		H 1100	Classes pers	H 1935
		H 1103	Ethnic groups	H 1935
		H 1105	Corp bodies	H 1935
		H 1110	Indiv pers	H 1935
		H 1120	Families	H 1935
		H 1140	Places	H 1935
		H 1155.6	Lit works/Auth	H 1935
–Picture Bibles	v	H 1188	Sacred works	
–Planning	x	H 1095	see *SCM:SH*	
		H 1105	Corp bodies	
		H 1151.5	Types schools	
		H 1153	Industries	
–Planting *(May Subd Geog)*	x	H 1180	Plants & crops	
–Planting time *(May Subd Geog)*	x	H 1180	Plants & crops	
–Plastic properties	x	H 1158	Materials	
–Platforms	v	H 1105	Corp bodies	
–Pneumatic equipment	x	H 1195	Land vehicles	
–Poetic works	x	H 1110	Indiv pers	

SUBDIVISION	SUBFIELD CODE(S)	FREE-FLOATING LIST IN SCM:SH	CATEGORY	USAGE GUIDELINES IN SCM:SH
–Poetry	v	H 1095	see *SCM:SH*	H 1800
		H 1100	Classes pers	H 1800
		H 1103	Ethnic groups	H 1800
		H 1105	Corp bodies	H 1800
		H 1110	Indiv pers	H 1800
		H 1120	Families	H 1800
		H 1140	Places	H 1800
–Polish authors	x	H 1156	Literatures	
–Polish influences	x	H 1156	Literatures	H 1675
–Political activity	x	H 1095	see *SCM:SH*	H 1942
		H 1100	Classes pers	H 1942
		H 1105	Corp bodies	H 1942
		H 1110	Indiv pers	H 1942
		H 1120	Families	H 1942
		H 1153	Industries	H 1942
		H 1155.2	Groups lit auth	H 1942
		H 1159	Military srvces	H 1942
		H 1187	Christian denom	H 1942
–Political and social views	x	H 1110	Indiv pers	
		H 1155.2	Groups lit auth	
–Political aspects *(May Subd Geog)*	x	H 1095	see *SCM:SH*	H 1942
		H 1185	Religions	H 1942
–Political-military affairs officers	x	H 1159	Military srvces	
–Politics and government	x	H 1103	Ethnic groups	H 1942
		H 1140	Places	H 1942
–Politics and government–16th century	x–y	H 1103	Ethnic groups	H 1942
		H 1140	Places	H 1942
–Politics and government–17th century	x–y	H 1103	Ethnic groups	H 1942
		H 1140	Places	H 1942
–Politics and government–18th century	x–y	H 1103	Ethnic groups	H 1942
		H 1140	Places	H 1942
–Politics and government–19th century	x–y	H 1103	Ethnic groups	H 1942
		H 1140	Places	H 1942
–Politics and government–20th century	x–y	H 1103	Ethnic groups	H 1942
		H 1140	Places	H 1942

SUBDIVISION	SUBFIELD CODE(S)	FREE-FLOATING LIST IN SCM:SH	CATEGORY	USAGE GUIDELINES IN SCM:SH
–Politics and government–21st century	x–y	H 1103 H 1140	Ethnic groups Places	H 1942 H 1942
–Politics and government–[period subdivision]–Philosophy	x–y–x	H 1140	Places	
–Politics and government–Philosophy	x–x	H 1140	Places	
–Pollen *(May Subd Geog)*	x	H 1180	Plants & crops	
–Pollen–Morphology	x–x	H 1180	Plants & crops	
–Pollen management *(May Subd Geog)*	x	H 1180	Plants & crops	
–Pollination *(May Subd Geog)*	x	H 1180	Plants & crops	
–Pollution control devices	x	H 1195	Land vehicles	
–Pollution control devices–Law and legislation *(May Subd Geog)*	x–x	H 1195	Land vehicles	
–Polysemy	x	H 1154	Languages	
–Popular works	v	H 1095 H 1154.5	see *SCM:SH* Legal topics	H 1943.5 H 1943.5
–Population	x	H 1103 H 1140 H 1149.5	Ethnic groups Places Colonies	
–Population–Economic aspects	x–x	H 1140	Places	
–Population–Environmental aspects	x–x	H 1140	Places	
–Population policy	x	H 1140	Places	
–Population regeneration *(May Subd Geog)*	x	H 1180	Plants & crops	
–Population viability analysis *(May Subd Geog)*	x	H 1147 H 1180	Animals Plants	

SUBDIVISION	SUBFIELD CODE(S)	FREE-FLOATING LIST IN SCM:SH	CATEGORY	USAGE GUIDELINES IN SCM:SH
–Portraits	v	H 1100	Classes pers	H 1935
		H 1103	Ethnic groups	H 1935
		H 1110	Indiv pers	H 1935
		H 1120	Families	H 1935
		H 1186	Relig orders	H 1935
		H 1200	Wars	H 1935
–Portuguese influences	x	H 1156	Literatures	H 1675
–Positions	x	H 1105	Corp bodies	
–Possessives	x	H 1154	Languages	
–Postal clerks	x	H 1159	Military srvces	
–Postal service	x	H 1159	Military srvces	
		H 1200	Wars	
–Postcolonial criticism *(May Subd Geog)*	x	H 1188	Sacred works	
–Poster collections	x	H 1105	Corp bodies	H 1427
		H 1110	Indiv pers	H 1427
		H 1120	Families	H 1427
–Posters	v	H 1095	see *SCM:SH*	H 1945.5
		H 1100	Classes pers	H 1945.5
		H 1103	Ethnic groups	H 1945.5
		H 1105	Corp bodies	H 1945.5
		H 1110	Indiv pers	H 1945.5
		H 1140	Places	H 1945.5
–Postharvest diseases and injuries *(May Subd Geog)*	x	H 1180	Plants & crops	
–Postharvest diseases and injuries– Biological control *(May Subd Geog)*	x–x	H 1180	Plants & crops	
–Postharvest diseases and injuries– Integrated control *(May Subd Geog)*	x–x	H 1180	Plants & crops	
–Postharvest losses *(May Subd Geog)*	x	H 1180	Plants & crops	
–Postharvest losses–Prevention	x–x	H 1180	Plants & crops	

SUBDIVISION	SUBFIELD CODE(S)	FREE-FLOATING LIST IN SCM:SH	CATEGORY	USAGE GUIDELINES IN SCM:SH
–Postharvest physiology *(May Subd Geog)*	x	H 1180	Plants & crops	
–Postharvest technology *(May Subd Geog)*	x	H 1180	Plants & crops	
–Postpositions	x	H 1154	Languages	
–Power supply *(May Subd Geog)*	x	H 1095 H 1153	see *SCM:SH* Industries	
–Power trains *(May Subd Geog)*	x	H 1195	Land vehicles	
–Power utilization	x	H 1145.5	Bodies water	
–Powers and duties	x	H 1155	Legis bodies	
–Practice *(May Subd Geog)*	x	H 1095	see *SCM:SH*	
–Prayers	v	H 1151.5 H 1188	Types schools Sacred works	
–Prayers–History and criticism	x–x	H 1188	Sacred works	
–Prayers and devotions	v	H 1095 H 1100 H 1103 H 1110 H 1185 H 1186 H 1187	see *SCM:SH* Classes pers Ethnic groups Indiv pers Religions Relig orders Christian denom	
–Prayers and devotions–History and criticism	x–x	H 1095 H 1100 H 1103 H 1110 H 1185 H 1186 H 1187	see *SCM:SH* Classes pers Ethnic groups Indiv pers Religions Relig orders Christian denom	
–Pre-existence	x	H 1110	Indiv pers	
–Precancerous conditions *(May Subd Geog)*	x	H 1165	Organs of body	
–Precooling *(May Subd Geog)*	x	H 1180	Plants & crops	
–Predators of *(May Subd Geog)*	x	H 1147	Animals	

SUBDIVISION	SUBFIELD CODE(S)	FREE-FLOATING LIST IN SCM:SH	CATEGORY	USAGE GUIDELINES IN SCM:SH
–Predators of–Control *(May Subd Geog)*	x–x	H 1147	Animals	
–Predators of–Ecology *(May Subd Geog)*	x–x	H 147	Animals	
–Prefaces	v	H 1188	Sacred works	
–Pregnancy *(May Subd Geog)*	x	H 1147	Animals	
–Preharvest sprouting *(May Subd Geog)*	x	H 1180	Plants & crops	
–Prepositional phrases	x	H 1154	Languages	
–Prepositions	x	H 1154	Languages	
–Preservation *(May Subd Geog)*	x	H 1095 H 1164 H 1180	see *SCM:SH* Organs of body Plants & crops	
–Presidents	x	H 1105	Corp bodies	
–Presiding officers	x	H 1155	Legis bodies	
–Press coverage *(May Subd Geog)*	x	H 1095 H 1100 H 1103 H 1105 H 1140 H 1200	see *SCM:SH* Classes pers Ethnic groups Corp bodies Places Wars	
–Prevention	x	H 1095 H 1150	see *SCM:SH* Diseases	
–Prevention–Needs assessment *(May Subd Geog)*	x–x	H 1150	Diseases	
–Prices *(May Subd Geog)*	x	H 1095 H 1149 H 1153 H 1158 H 1180 H 1195	see *SCM:SH* Chemicals Industries Materials Plants & crops Land vehicles	
–Prices–Government policy *(May Subd Geog)*	x–x	H 1095 H 1153	see *SCM:SH* Industries	

SUBDIVISION	SUBFIELD CODE(S)	FREE-FLOATING LIST IN SCM:SH	CATEGORY	USAGE GUIDELINES IN SCM:SH
–Prices–Law and legislation *(May Subd Geog)*	x–x	H 1153 H 1195	Industries Land vehicles	
–Prisoners and prisons	x	H 1200	Wars	
–Prisoners and prisons, British, [German, etc.]	x	H 1200	Wars	
–Prisons	x	H 1159	Military srvces	
–Private bills	v	H 1155	Legis bodies	
–Private collections *(May Subd Geog)*	x	H 1095	see *SCM:SH*	H 1427
–Privatization *(May Subd Geog)*	x	H 1153	Industries	
–Privileges and immunities	x	H 1095 H 1105 H 1151.5 H 1155	see *SCM:SH* Corp bodies Types schools Legis bodies	
–Prizes, etc.	x	H 1200	Wars	
–Problems, exercises, etc.	v	H 1095	see *SCM:SH*	
–Processing *(May Subd Geog)*	x	H 1147 H 1180	Animals Plants & crops	
–Processing–Machinery *(May Subd Geog)*	x–x	H 1180	Plants & crops	
–Procurement	x	H 1105 H 1159	Corp bodies Military srvces	
–Production and direction *(May Subd Geog)*	x x	H 1095 H 1160	see *SCM:SH* Musical comps	
–Production control *(May Subd Geog)*	x	H 1095 H 1153	see *SCM:SH* Industries	
–Production standards *(May Subd Geog)*	x	H 1095 H 1153	see *SCM:SH* Industries	
–Productivity *(May Subd Geog)*	x	H 1147	Animals	
–Professional ethics *(May Subd Geog)*	x	H 1100	Classes pers	H 1949

SUBDIVISION	SUBFIELD CODE(S)	FREE-FLOATING LIST IN SCM:SH	CATEGORY	USAGE GUIDELINES IN SCM:SH
–Professional relationships *(May Subd Geog)*	x	H 1100	Classes pers	
–Professional staff	x	H 1151 H 1151.5	Indiv schools Types schools	
–Prognosis *(May Subd Geog)*	x	H 1150	Diseases	
–Programmed instruction	v	H 1095	see *SCM:SH*	
–Programming *(May Subd Geog)*	x	H 1095	see *SCM:SH*	
–Promotions	x	H 1159	Military srvces	
–Promotions *(May Subd Geog)*	x	H 1100 H 1103	Classes pers Ethnic groups	
–Pronominals	x	H 1154	Languages	
–Pronoun	x	H 1154	Languages	
–Pronunciation	x	H 1154	Languages	
–Pronunciation by foreign speakers	x	H 1154	Languages	
–Propaganda	x	H 1200	Wars	
–Propagation *(May Subd Geog)*	x	H 1180	Plants & crops	
–Prophecies	x	H 1095 H 1100 H 1103 H 1110 H 1188 H 1200	see *SCM:SH* Classes pers Ethnic groups Indiv pers Sacred works Wars	
–Prophecies–Chronology	x–v	H 1188	Sacred works	
–Prophecies–[subject of prophecy]	x–x	H 1188	Sacred works	
–Prose	x	H 1110	Indiv pers	
–Prosodic analysis	x	H 1154	Languages	

SUBDIVISION	SUBFIELD CODE(S)	FREE-FLOATING LIST IN SCM:SH	CATEGORY	USAGE GUIDELINES IN SCM:SH
–Protection *(May Subd Geog)*	x	H 1095	see *SCM:SH*	
		H 1100	Classes pers	
		H 1164	Organs of body	
		H 1180	Plants & crops	
		H 1195	Land vehicles	
–Protection–Law and legislation *(May Subd Geog)*	x–x	H 1180	Plants and crops	
–Protest movements *(May Subd Geog)*	x	H 1200	Wars	
–Protestant authors	x	H 1156	Literatures	
–Provenance trials *(May Subd Geog)*	x	H 1180	Plants & crops	
–Provenances *(May Subd Geog)*	x	H 1180	Plants & crops	
–Provençal influences	x	H 1156	Literatures	H 1675
–Provinces	x	H 1095	see *SCM:SH*	H 713
–Provincialisms *(May Subd Geog)*	x	H 1154	Languages	
–Provisioning	x	H 1159	Military srvces	
–Pruning *(May Subd Geog)*	x	H 1180	Plants & crops	
–Psychic aspects *(May Subd Geog)*	x	H 1147	Animals	
		H 1180	Plants & crops	
–Psychological aspects	x	H 1095	see *SCM:SH*	
		H 1147	Animals	
		H 1150	Diseases	
		H 1200	Wars	
–Psychological testing *(May Subd Geog)*	x	H 1100	Classes pers	H 2186
		H 1103	Ethnic groups	H 2186
		H 1147	Animals	
–Psychology	x	H 1095	see *SCM:SH*	
		H 1100	Classes pers	
		H 1103	Ethnic groups	
		H 1110	Indiv pers	
		H 1147	Animals	
		H 1185	Religions	
		H 1188	Sacred works	

SUBDIVISION	SUBFIELD CODE(S)	FREE-FLOATING LIST IN SCM:SH	CATEGORY	USAGE GUIDELINES IN SCM:SH
–Psychophysiology	x	H 1164	Organs of body	
–Psychosomatic aspects *(May Subd Geog)*	x	H 1150	Diseases	
–Psychotropic effects *(May Subd Geog)*	x	H 1149	Chemicals	
–Public opinion	x	H 1095	see *SCM:SH*	H 1955
		H 1100	Classes pers	H 1955
		H 1103	Ethnic groups	H 1955
		H 1105	Corp bodies	H 1955
		H 1110	Indiv pers	H 1955
		H 1200	Wars	H 1955
–Public records	x	H 1105	Corp bodies	
–Public relations *(May Subd Geog)*	x	H 1095	see *SCM:SH*	
		H 1105	Corp bodies	
		H 1159	Military srvces	
–Public services	x	H 1151	Indiv schools	
		H 1151.5	Types schools	
–Public welfare *(May Subd Geog)*	x	H 1103	Ethnic groups	
–Publication and distribution *(May Subd Geog)*	x	H 1188	Sacred works	
–Publication of proceedings	x	H 1155	Legis bodies	
–Publishing *(May Subd Geog)*	x	H 1095	see *SCM:SH*	
		H 1105	Corp bodies	
		H 1156	Literatures	
		H 1187	Christian denom	
–Pump placing *(May Subd Geog)*	x	H 1158	Materials	
–Punctuation	x	H 1154	Languages	
–Purchasing *(May Subd Geog)*	x	H 1095	see *SCM:SH*	
		H 1147	Animals	
–Purges	x	H 1105	Corp bodies	
–Purification *(May Subd Geog)*	x	H 1149	Chemicals	
–Puritan authors	x	H 1156	Literatures	

SUBDIVISION	SUBFIELD CODE(S)	FREE-FLOATING LIST IN SCM:SH	CATEGORY	USAGE GUIDELINES IN SCM:SH
–Quaker authors	x	H 1156	Literatures	
–Qualifications	x	H 1155	Legis bodies	
–Quality *(May Subd Geog)*	x	H 1147	Animals	
		H 1180	Plants & crops	
–Quality control	x	H 1095	see *SCM:SH*	
		H 1153	Industries	
		H 1158	Materials	
–Quantifiers	x	H 1154	Languages	
–Quantity	x	H 1154	Languages	
–Queens	x	H 1103	Ethnic groups	
–Quenching *(May Subd Geog)*	x	H 1149	Chemicals	
		H 1158	Materials	
–Qin-Han dynasties, 221 B.C.- 220 A.D.	y	H 1148	Chinese art	
–Quotations	v	H 1100	Classes pers	H 1969
		H 1103	Ethnic groups	H 1969
		H 1110	Indiv pers	H 1969
		H 1120	Families	H 1969
		H 1188	Sacred works	H 1969
–Quotations, Early	x	H 1188	Sacred works	
–Quotations in rabbinical literature	x	H 1188	Sacred works	
–Quotations in the New Testament	x	H 1188	Sacred works	
–Quotations, maxims, etc.	v	H 1095	see *SCM:SH*	H 1969
		H 1140	Places	H 1969
–Race identity *(May Subd Geog)*	x	H 1103	Ethnic groups	
–Race relations	x	H 1140	Places	
		H 1149.5	Colonies	
–Race relations–Economic aspects	x–x	H 1140	Places	
–Race relations–Political aspects	x–x	H 1140	Places	

SUBDIVISION	SUBFIELD CODE(S)	FREE-FLOATING LIST IN SCM:SH	CATEGORY	USAGE GUIDELINES IN SCM:SH
–Racial analysis *(May Subd Geog)*	x	H 1147	Animals	
–Radar	x	H 1200	Wars	
–Radiation injuries *(May Subd Geog)*	x	H 1164	Organs of body	
–Radiation preservation *(May Subd Geog)*	x	H 1180	Plants & crops	
–Radiator ornaments	x	H 1195	Land vehicles	
–Radiators	x	H 1195	Land vehicles	
–Radio and television plays	x	H 1110	Indiv pers	
–Radio broadcasting and the war, [revolution, etc.]	x	H 1200	Wars	
–Radio broadcasting of proceedings	x	H 1155	Legis bodies	
–Radio equipment	x	H 1195	Land vehicles	
–Radio equipment–Security measures *(May Subd Geog)*	x–x	H 1195	Land vehicles	
–Radio installations	x	H 1159	Military srvces	
–Radio tracking *(May Subd Geog)*	x	H 1147	Animals	
–Radioactive contamination *(May Subd Geog)*	x	H 1180	Plants & crops	
–Radiography *(May Subd Geog)*	x	H 1158 H 1164 H 1180	Materials Organs of body Plants & crops	
–Radiography–Law and legislation *(May Subd Geog)*	x–x	H 1164	Organs of body	
–Radiography–Positioning *(May Subd Geog)*	x–x	H 1164	Organs of body	
–Radioimmunoimaging *(May Subd Geog)*	x	H 1150	Diseases	
–Radioimmunotherapy *(May Subd Geog)*	x	H 1150	Diseases	

SUBDIVISION	SUBFIELD CODE(S)	FREE-FLOATING LIST IN SCM:SH	CATEGORY	USAGE GUIDELINES IN SCM:SH
–Radioiodination *(May Subd Geog)*	x	H 1149	Chemicals	
–Radiomen	x	H 1159	Military srvces	
–Radionuclide imaging *(May Subd Geog)*	x	H 1150 H 1164	Diseases Organs of body	
–Radiotherapy *(May Subd Geog)*	x	H 1150	Diseases	
–Radiotherapy–Complications *(May Subd Geog)*	x–x	H 1150	Diseases	
–Rapid solidification processing *(May Subd Geog)*	x	H 1158	Materials	
–Rates *(May Subd Geog)*	x	H 1095	see *SCM:SH*	
–Rating of *(May Subd Geog)*	x	H 1100	Classes pers	
–Ratings and rankings *(May Subd Geog)*	x	H 1151.5	Types schools	
–Reactivity *(May Subd Geog)*	x	H 1149	Chemicals	
–Reader-response criticism	x	H 1188	Sacred books	
–Readers	v	H 1154	Languages	H 1975
–Readers–[form]	v–v	H 1154	Languages	H 1975
–Readers–[topic]	v–x	H 1154	Languages	H 1975
–Readers for new literates	v	H 1154	Languages	
–Reading *(May Subd Geog)*	x	H 1188	Sacred works	
–Receptors	x	H 1149	Chemicals	
–Receptors–Effect of drugs on *(May Subd Geog)*	x–x	H 1149	Chemicals	
–Recolonization *(May Subd Geog)*	x	H 1147	Animals	
–Reconaissance operations	x	H 1200	Wars	
–Reconaissance operations, American, [German, etc.]	x	H 1200	Wars	

SUBDIVISION	SUBFIELD CODE(S)	FREE-FLOATING LIST IN SCM:SH	CATEGORY	USAGE GUIDELINES IN SCM:SH
–Records and correspondence	v	H 1095 H 1105 H 1153 H 1159	see *SCM:SH* Corp bodies Industries Military srvces	
–Recreation *(May Subd Geog)*	x	H 1100 H 1103	Classes pers Ethnic groups	
–Recreational use *(May Subd Geog)*	x	H 1095	see *SCM:SH*	
–Recruiting *(May Subd Geog)*	x	H 1100	Classes pers	
–Recruiting, enlistment, etc.	x	H 1159	Military srvces	
–Recruiting, enlistment, etc.–Revolution, 1775-1783, [Spanish-American War, 1898, etc.	x–y	H 1159	Military srvces	
–Recruiting, enlistment, etc.–Law and legislation	x–x	H 1159	Military srvces	
–Recycling *(May Subd Geog)*	x	H 1149 H 1158	Chemicals Materials	
–Reduplication	x	H 1154	Languages	
–Reference	x	H 1154	Languages	
–Reference books	x	H 1095	see *SCM:SH*	
–Reference editions	v	H 1188	Sacred works	
–Refining *(May Subd Geog)*	x	H 1158	Materials	
–Reflexives	x	H 1154	Languages	
–Reform	x	H 1154 H 1155	Languages Legis bodies	
–Refugees *(May Subd Geog)*	x	H 1200	Wars	
–Regeneration *(May Subd Geog)*	x	H 1164 H 1180	Organs of body Plants & crops	
–Regimental histories *(May Subd Geog)*	x	H 1200	Wars	H 1995

SUBDIVISION	SUBFIELD CODE(S)	FREE-FLOATING LIST IN SCM:SH	CATEGORY	USAGE GUIDELINES IN SCM:SH
–Regional disparities	x	H 1095	see *SCM:SH*	
–Regions	x	H 1095	see *SCM:SH*	H 713
–Registers	v	H 1095	see *SCM:SH*	H 1558
		H 1100	Classes pers	H 1558
		H 1103	Ethnic groups	H 1558
		H 1105	Corp bodies	H 1558
		H 1120	Families	H 1558
		H 1140	Places	H 1558
		H 1159	Military srvces	H 1558
		H 1200	Wars	H 1558
–Registers of dead	v	H 1159	Military srvces	
–Registers of dead *(May Subd Geog)*	v	H 1200	Wars	
–Registration and transfer *(May Subd Geog)*	x	H 1195	Land vehicles	
–Registration and transfer–Fees *(May Subd Geog)*	x–x	H 1195	Land vehicles	
–Regulation	x	H 1145.5	Bodies water	
–Regulations	v	H 1151	Indiv schools	
		H 1159	Military srvces	
–Rehabilitation *(May Subd Geog)*	x	H 1100	Classes pers	
		H 1103	Ethnic groups	
–Reimplantation *(May Subd Geog)*	x	H 1164	Organs of body	
–Reinstatement *(May Subd Geog)*	x	H 1100	Classes pers	
–Reintroduction *(May Subd Geog)*	x	H 1147	Animals	
		H 1180	Plants & crops	
–Relapse *(May Subd Geog)*	x	H 1150	Diseases	
–Relation to Matthew, [Jeremiah, etc.]	x	H 1188	Sacred works	
–Relation to the Old Testament	x	H 1188	Sacred works	
–Relational grammar	x	H 1154	Languages	

Free-floating Subdivisions: An Alphabetical Index

SUBDIVISION	SUBFIELD CODE(S)	FREE-FLOATING LIST IN SCM:SH	CATEGORY	USAGE GUIDELINES IN SCM:SH
–Relations	x	H 1185 H 1187	Religions Christian denom	
–Relations *(May Subd Geog)*	x	H 1140	Places	H 1996
–Relations–Anglican Communion, [Lutheran Church, etc.]	x–x	H 1187	Christian denom	
–Relations–Buddhism, [Judaism, etc.]	x–x	H 1187	Christian denom	
–Relations–Christianity, [Islam, etc.]	x–x	H 1185	Religions	
–Relations–Evangelicalism	x–x	H 1187	Christian denom	
–Relations–Foreign countries	x–z	H 1140	Places	H 1996
–Relations–Protestant churches	x–x	H 1187	Christian denom	
–Relations with [specific class of persons or ethnic group]	x	H 1110	Indiv pers	
–Relations with men	x	H 1110 H 1155.2	Indiv pers Groups lit auth	
–Relations with women	x	H 1110 H 1155.2	Indiv pers Groups lit auth	
–Relative clauses	x	H 1154	Languages	
–Reliability	x	H 1095	see *SCM:SH*	
–Relics *(May Subd Geog)*	x	H 1110 H 1120	Indiv pers Families	
–Relief models	v	H 1140	Places	
–Religion	x	H 1103 H 1105 H 1110 H 1140 H 1149.5 H 1151.5	Ethnic groups Corp bodies Indiv pers Places Colonies Types schools	H 1997 H 1997 H 1997 H 1997 H 1997 H 1997
–Religion–16th century	x–y	H 1140	Places	H 1997
–Religion–17th century	x–y	H 1140	Places	H 1997

SUBDIVISION	SUBFIELD CODE(S)	FREE-FLOATING LIST IN SCM:SH	CATEGORY	USAGE GUIDELINES IN SCM:SH
–Religion–18th century	x–y	H 1140	Places	H 1997
–Religion–19th century	x–y	H 1140	Places	H 1997
–Religion–20th century	x–y	H 1140	Places	H 1997
–Religion–21st century	x–y	H 1140	Places	H 1997
–Religion–Economic aspects	x–x	H 1140	Places	
–Religious aspects	x	H 1147	Animals	H 1998
		H 1149	Chemicals	H 1998
		H 1150	Diseases	H 1998
		H 1154	Languages	H 1998
		H 1158	Materials	H 1998
		H 1160	Musical comps	H 1998
		H 1161	Musical instrum	H 1998
		H 1164	Organs of body	H 1998
		H 1180	Plants & crops	H 1998
		H 1200	Wars	H 1998
–Religious aspects–Baptists, [Catholic Church, etc.]	x–x	H 1150	Diseases	H 1998
		H 1154	Languages	H 1998
		H 1160	Musical comps	H 1998
		H 1161	Musical instrum	H 1998
		H 1180	Plants & crops	H 1998
		H 1200	Wars	H 1998
–Religious aspects–Buddhism, [Christianity, etc.]	x–x	H 1147	Animals	H 1998
		H 1149	Chemicals	H 1998
		H 1150	Diseases	H 1998
		H 1154	Languages	H 1998
		H 1158	Materials	H 1998
		H 1160	Musical comps	H 1998
		H 1161	Musical instrum	H 1998
		H 1164	Organs of body	H 1998
		H 1180	Plants & crops	H 1998
		H 1200	Wars	H 1998
–Religious aspects–Protestant churches	x–x	H 1200	Wars	H 1998
–Religious life	x	H 1159	Military srvces	H 2015.5
–Religious life (May Subd Geog)	x	H 1100	Classes pers	H 2015.5
–Religious life and customs	x	H 1140	Places	H 2016
		H 1149.5	Colonies	H 2016

SUBDIVISION	SUBFIELD CODE(S)	FREE-FLOATING LIST IN SCM:SH	CATEGORY	USAGE GUIDELINES IN SCM:SH
–Relocation *(May Subd Geog)*	x	H 1103 H 1100	Ethnic groups Classes pers	
–Remedial teaching *(May Subd Geog)*	x	H 1154	Languages	
–Remodeling *(May Subd Geog)*	x	H 1095	see *SCM:SH*	
–Remodeling for other use *(May Subd Geog)*	x	H 1095	see *SCM:SH*	
–Remote sensing	x	H 1095	see *SCM:SH*	
–Remote-sensing images	v	H 1140	Places	
–Remote-sensing maps	v	H 1095 H 1140	see *SCM:SH* Places	
–Remount service	x	H 1159	Military srvces	
–Reoperation *(May Subd Geog)*	x	H 1150 H 1164	Diseases Organs of body	
–Reorganization	x	H 1105 H 1159	Corp bodies Military srvces	
–Repairing *(May Subd Geog)*	x	H 1095	see *SCM:SH*	
–Reparations	x	H 1200	Wars	
–Reparations *(May Subd Geog)*	x	H 1103	Ethnic groups	
–Repatriation of war dead *(May Subd Geog)*	x	H 1200	Wars	
–Reporters and reporting	x	H 1155	Legis bodies	
–Reporting *(May Subd Geog)*	x	H 1150	Diseases	
–Reporting to *(May Subd Geog)*	x	H 1100	Classes pers	
–Reproduction	x	H 1147 H 1148 H 1180	Animals Art Plants & crops	
–Reproduction–Climatic factors *(May Subd Geog)*	x–x	H 1147	Animals	

SUBDIVISION	SUBFIELD CODE(S)	FREE-FLOATING LIST IN SCM:SH	CATEGORY	USAGE GUIDELINES IN SCM:SH
–Reproduction–Effect of altitude on *(May Subd Geog)*	x–x	H 1147	Animals	
–Reproduction–Effect of light on *(May Subd Geog)*	x–x	H 1147	Animals	
–Reproduction–Effect of temperature on *(May Subd Geog)*	x–x	H 1147	Animals	
–Reproduction–Endocrine aspects	x–x	H 1147	Animals	
–Reproduction–Regulation	x–x	H 1147	Animals	
–Republics	x	H 1095	see *SCM:SH*	H 713
–Research *(May Subd Geog)*	x	H 1095	see *SCM:SH*	H 2020
		H 1100	Classes pers	H 2020
		H 1103	Ethnic groups	H 2020
		H 1105	Corp bodies	H 2020
		H 1140	Places	H 2020
		H 1149	Chemicals	H 2020
		H 1154.5	Legal topics	H 2020
		H 1180	Plants & crops	H 2020
–Research–Law and legislation *(May Subd Geog)*	x–x	H 1149	Chemicals	
		H 1180	Plants & crops	
–Research grants	x	H 1105	Corp bodies	
–Research grants *(May Subd Geog)*	x	H 1095	see *SCM:SH*	
–Reserve fleets	x	H 1159	Military srvces	
–Reserves	x	H 1159	Military srvces	
–Reserves–Pay, allowances, etc.	x–x	H 1159	Military srvces	
–Reserves–Personnel records	x–x	H 1159	Military srvces	
–Reserves–Promotions	x–x	H 1159	Military srvces	
–Residence requirements *(May Subd Geog)*	x	H 1100	Classes pers	
		H 1151.5	Types schools	
–Residues *(May Subd Geog)*	x	H 1180	Plants & crops	
–Resignation *(May Subd Geog)*	x	H 1100	Classes pers	

SUBDIVISION	SUBFIELD CODE(S)	FREE-FLOATING LIST IN SCM:SH	CATEGORY	USAGE GUIDELINES IN SCM:SH
–Resignation from office	x	H 1110	Indiv pers	
–Resolutions	v	H 1155	Legis bodies	
–Respiration *(May Subd Geog)*	x	H 1147	Animals	
–Respiratory organs	x	H 1147	Animals	
–Respite care *(May Subd Geog)*	x	H 1100 H 1103	Classes pers Ethnic groups	
–Restoration, 1660-1700	y	H 1156	Drama	
–Resultative constructions	x	H 1154	Languages	
–Retarders *(May Subd Geog)*	x	H 1195	Land vehicles	
–Retirement *(May Subd Geog)*	x	H 1100 H 1103	Classes pers Ethnic groups	
–Reverse indexes	v	H 1154	Languages	
–Reviews	v	H 1095	see *SCM:SH*	H 2021
–Revival	x	H 1154	Languages	
–Rhetoric	x	H 1154	Languages	
–Rhyme	x	H 1154	Languages	
–Rhythm	x	H 1154	Languages	
–Riding qualities *(May Subd Geog)*	x	H 1195	Land vehicles	
–Riot, [date]	x	H 1151	Indiv schools	
–Riots	x	H 1151	Indiv schools	
–Ripening *(May Subd Geog)*	x	H 1180	Plants & crops	
–Risk assessment *(May Subd Geog)*	x	H 1095	see *SCM:SH*	
–Risk factors *(May Subd Geog)*	x	H 1150	Diseases	
–Risk management *(May Subd Geog)*	x	H 1153	Industries	
–Rites and ceremonies	x	H 1103	Ethnic groups	

SUBDIVISION	SUBFIELD CODE(S)	FREE-FLOATING LIST IN SCM:SH	CATEGORY	USAGE GUIDELINES IN SCM:SH
–Rituals	x	H 1105 H 1185	Corp bodies Religions	
–Rituals–Texts	x–v	H 1185	Religions	H 2190
–Rituals–Texts–Concordances	x–x–v	H 1185	Religions	
–Rituals–Texts–History and criticism	x–x–x	H 1185	Religions	
–Riverine operations *(May Subd Geog)*	x	H 1200	Wars	
–Riverine operations, American, [British, etc.] *(May Subd Geog)*	x	H 1200	Wars	
–Rollover protective structures *(May Subd Geog)*	x	H 1195	Land vehicles	
–Roman influences	x	H 1156	Literatures	H 1675
–Romances	v	H 1095 H 1110	see *SCM:SH* Indiv pers	H 1795 H 1795
–Romanian influences	x	H 1156	Literatures	H 1675
–Roots	x	H 1154 H 1180	Languages Plants & crops	
–Roots–Anatomy	x–x	H 1180	Plants & crops	
–Roots–Diseases and pests *(May Subd Geog)*	x–x	H 1180	Plants & crops	
–Roots–Physiology *(May Subd Geog)*	x–x	H 1180	Plants & crops	
–Rootstocks *(May Subd Geog)*	x	H 1180	Plants & crops	
–Rowing	x	H 1151	Indiv schools	
–Rugby football	x	H 1151	Indiv schools	
–Rules	v	H 1095 H 1186	see *SCM:SH* Relig orders	
–Rules and practice	v	H 1095 H 1105	see *SCM:SH* Corp bodies	

SUBDIVISION	SUBFIELD CODE(S)	FREE-FLOATING LIST IN SCM:SH	CATEGORY	USAGE GUIDELINES IN SCM:SH
–Rum ration	x	H 1159	Military srvces	
–Rupture *(May Subd Geog)*	x	H 1164	Organs of body	
–Rural conditions	x	H 1140	Places	
		H 1149.5	Colonies	
–Russian influences	x	H 1156	Literatures	H 1675
–Sacred books	v	H 1185	Religions	
–Sacred books–Hermeneutics	x–x	H 1185	Religions	
–Sacred books–Introductions	x–v	H 1185	Religions	
–Sacred books–Language, style	x–x	H 1185	Religions	
–Sacred books–Preservation *(May Subd Geog)*	x–x	H 1185	Religions	
–Sacred books–Quotations	x–v	H 1185	Religions	
–Safety appliances *(May Subd Geog)*	x	H 1095	see *SCM:SH*	
		H 1195	Land vehicles	
–Safety measures	x	H 1095	see *SCM:SH*	
		H 1151.5	Types schools	
		H 1153	Industries	
		H 1159	Military srvces	
–Safety regulations *(May Subd Geog)*	x	H 1095	see *SCM:SH*	H 1705
		H 1153	Industries	H 1705
–Sailors' handbooks	v	H 1159	Military srvces	
–Salaries, etc.	x	H 1155	Legis bodies	
–Salaries, etc. *(May Subd Geog)*	x	H 1100	Classes pers	
–Salaries, etc.–Cost-of-living adjustments *(May Subd Geog)*	x–x	H 1100	Classes pers	
–Salaries, etc.–Law and legislation *(May Subd Geog)*	x–x	H 1100	Classes pers	
–Sampling *(May Subd Geog)*	x	H 1149	Chemicals	
		H 1158	Materials	
		H 1180	Plants & crops	

SUBDIVISION	SUBFIELD CODE(S)	FREE-FLOATING LIST IN SCM:SH	CATEGORY	USAGE GUIDELINES IN SCM:SH
—Sanitary affairs	x	H 1151 H 1151.5 H 1159	Indiv schools Types schools Military srvces	
—Sanitation	x	H 1105	Corp bodies	
—Sanitation (May Subd Geog)	x	H 1095 H 1153	see SCM:SH Industries	
—Sanskrit influences	x	H 1156	Literatures	H 1675
—Scandinavian influences	x	H 1156	Literatures	H 1675
—Scenarios	v	H 1160	Musical comps	
—Scheduled tribes	x	H 1140	Places	
—Scholarships, fellowships, etc. (May Subd Geog)	x	H 1095 H 1100 H 1103	see SCM:SH Classes pers Ethnic groups	
—Scholia	v	H 1110	Indiv pers	
—Schooling (May Subd Geog)	x	H 1147	Animals	
—Science (May Subd Geog)	x	H 1103 H 1200	Ethnic groups Wars	
—Scientific apparatus collections	x	H 1105 H 1110 H 1120	Corp bodies Indiv pers Families	H 1427 H 1427 H 1427
—Scientific applications (May Subd Geog)	x	H 1095	see SCM:SH	
—Scores	v	H 1160	Musical comps	
—Scores and parts	v	H 1160	Musical comps	
—Scores and parts (solo)	v	H 1160	Musical comps	
—Scottish authors	x	H 1156	Literatures	
—Scottish influences	x	H 1156	Literatures	H 1675
—Scouts and scouting	x	H 1200	Wars	
—Scrapping (May Subd Geog)	x	H 1195	Land vehicles	

SUBDIVISION	SUBFIELD CODE(S)	FREE-FLOATING LIST IN SCM:SH	CATEGORY	USAGE GUIDELINES IN SCM:SH
–Sea life	x	H 1159	Military srvces	
–Seal	x	H 1105	Corp bodies	
		H 1110	Indiv pers	
		H 1140	Places	
–Search and rescue operations *(May (Subd Geog)*	x	H 1159	Military srvces	
		H 1200	Wars	
–Seasonal distribution *(May Subd Geog)*	x	H 1147	Animals	
–Seasonal variations *(May Subd Geog)*	x	H 1147	Animals	
		H 1150	Diseases	
		H 1153	Industries	
		H 1180	Plants & crops	
–Seat belts	x	H 1195	Land vehicles	
–Seat belts–Law and legislation *(May Subd Geog)*	x–x	H 1195	Land vehicles	
–Seats *(May Subd Geog)*	x	H 1195	Land vehicles	
–Secret service *(May Subd Geog)*	x	H 1200	Wars	
–Secretion	x	H 1149	Chemicals	
–Secretion–Regulation	x–x	H 1149	Chemicals	
–Secretions	x	H 1164	Organs of body	
–Security measures	x	H 1105	Corp bodies	
		H 1159	Military srvces	
–Security measures *(May Subd Geog)*	x	H 1095	see *SCM:SH*	
		H 1151.5	Types schools	
		H 1153	Industries	
–Seedlings	x	H 1180	Plants & crops	
–Seedlings–Ecophysiology *(May Subd Geog)*	x–x	H 1180	Plants & crops	
–Seedlings–Effect of browsing on *(May Subd Geog)*	x–x	H 1180	Plants & crops	H 1580
–Seedlings–Evaluation	x–x	H 1180	Plants & crops	

SUBDIVISION	SUBFIELD CODE(S)	FREE-FLOATING LIST IN SCM:SH	CATEGORY	USAGE GUIDELINES IN SCM:SH
–Seedlings–Protection *(May Subd Geog)*	x–x	H 1180	Plants & crops	
–Seedlings–Quality *(May Subd Subd Geog)*	x–x	H 1180	Plants & crops	
–Seedlings–Roots	x–x	H 1180	Plants & crops	
–Seedlings, Bareroot	x	H 1180	Plants & crops	
–Seedlings, Container	x	H 1180	Plants & crops	
–Seeds *(May Subd Geog)*	x	H 1180	Plants & crops	
–Seeds–Anatomy	x–x	H 1180	Plants & crops	
–Seeds–Certification *(May Subd Geog)*	x–x	H 1180	Plants & crops	
–Seeds–Dispersal *(May Subd Geog)*	x–x	H 1180	Plants & crops	
–Seeds–Dormancy *(May Subd Geog)*	x–x	H 1180	Plants & crops	
–Seeds–Drying *(May Subd Geog)*	x–x	H 1180	Plants & crops	
–Seeds–Handling *(May Subd Geog)*	x–x	H 1180	Plants & crops	
–Seeds–Harvesting *(May Subd Geog)*	x–x	H 1180	Plants & crops	
–Seeds–Identification	x–v	H 1180	Plants & crops	
–Seeds–Marketing	x–x	H 1180	Plants & crops	
–Seeds–Morphology	x–x	H 1180	Plants & crops	
–Seeds–Packaging *(May Subd Geog)*	x–x	H 1180	Plants & crops	
–Seeds–Physiology *(May Subd Geog)*	x–x	H 1180	Plants & crops	
–Seeds–Postharvest technology *(May Subd Geog)*	x–x	H 1180	Plants & crops	
–Seeds–Predators of *(May Subd Geog)*	x–x	H 1180	Plants & crops	
–Seeds–Processing *(May Subd Geog)*	x–x	H 1180	Plants & crops	
–Seeds–Quality *(May Subd Geog)*	x–x	H 1180	Plants & crops	

SUBDIVISION	SUBFIELD CODE(S)	FREE-FLOATING LIST IN SCM:SH	CATEGORY	USAGE GUIDELINES IN SCM:SH
–Seeds–Storage *(May Subd Geog)*	x–x	H 1180	Plants & crops	
–Seeds–Testing	x–x	H 1180	Plants & crops	
–Seeds–Viability *(May Subd Geog)*	x–x	H 1180	Plants & crops	
–Selection *(May Subd Geog)*	x	H 1147 H 1180	Animals Plants & crops	
–Selection and appointment *(May Subd Geog)*	x	H 1100	Classes pers	
–Self-instruction	v	H 1154	Languages	
–Self-portraits	v	H 1110	Indiv pers	
–Self-regulation *(May Subd Geog)*	x	H 1153	Industries	
–Semantics	x	H 1154	Languages	
–Semantics, Historical	x	H 1154	Languages	
–Sense organs	x	H 1147	Animals	
–Sensory evaluation *(May Subd Geog)*	x	H 1180	Plants & crops	
–Sentences	x	H 1154	Languages	
–Separation *(May Subd Geog)*	x	H 1149	Chemicals	
–Serial numbers	x	H 1195	Land vehicles	
–Sermons	v	H 1095 H 1110 H 1151.5 H 1185 H 1187 H 1188 H 1200	see *SCM:SH* Indiv pers Types schools Religions Christian denom Sacred works Wars	H 2032 H 2032 H 2032 H 2032 H 2032 H 2032 H 2032
–Sermons–History and criticism	x–x	H 1185 H 1187	Religions Christian denom	H 2032 H 2032
–Sermons–Outlines, syllabi, etc.	x–v	H 1188	Sacred works	
–Serodiagnosis *(May Subd Geog)*	x	H 1150	Diseases	

SUBDIVISION	SUBFIELD CODE(S)	FREE-FLOATING LIST IN SCM:SH	CATEGORY	USAGE GUIDELINES IN SCM:SH
–Service clubs	x	H 1159	Military srvces	
–Service craft	x	H 1159	Military srvces	
–Service life *(May Subd Geog)*	x	H 1195	Land vehicles	
–Services for *(May Subd Geog)*	x	H 1100	Classes pers	
		H 1103	Ethnic groups	
		H 1147	Animals	
		H 1151.5	Types schools	
–Services for–Contracting out *(May Subd Geog)*	x–x	H 1151.5	Types schools	
–Settings	x	H 1110	Indiv pers	
–Sex differences *(May Subd Geog)*	x	H 1095	see *SCM:SH*	
		H 1154	Languages	
		H 1164	Organs of body	
–Sex factors *(May Subd Geog)*	x	H 1150	Diseases	
–Sexing *(May Subd Geog)*	x	H 1147	Animals	
–Sexual behavior	x	H 1110	Indiv pers	
–Sexual behavior *(May Subd Geog)*	x	H 1100	Classes pers	
		H 1103	Ethnic groups	
		H 1147	Animals	
–Shamanistic influences	x	H 1156	Literatures	H 1675
–Shelling *(May Subd Geog)*	x	H 1180	Plants & crops	
–Shelling–Machinery *(May Subd Geog)*	x–x	H 1180	Plants & crops	
–Shock absorbers	x	H 1195	Land vehicles	
–Shore patrol	x	H 1159	Military srvces	
–Showing *(May Subd Geog)*	x	H 1147	Animals	
		H 1180	Plants & crops	
–Shrines *(May Subd Geog)*	x	H 1110	Indiv pers	
–Side effects *(May Subd Geog)*	x	H 1149	Chemicals	

SUBDIVISION	SUBFIELD CODE(S)	FREE-FLOATING LIST IN SCM:SH	CATEGORY	USAGE GUIDELINES IN SCM:SH
–Signers	x	H 1095	see *SCM:SH*	
–Silage *(May Subd Geog)*	x	H 1180	Plants & crops	
–Silica content *(May Subd Geog)*	x	H 1180	Plants & crops	
–Simplified editions	v	H 1160	Musical comps	
–Simulation games	x	H 1095	see *SCM:SH*	
–Simulation methods	x	H 1095	see *SCM:SH*	H 2040
–Sindhi authors	x	H 1156	Literatures	
–Size *(May Subd Geog)*	x	H 1147	Animals	
		H 1164	Organs of body	
		H 1180	Plants & crops	
–Sizes *(May Subd Geog)*	x	H 1195	Land vehicles	
–Ski troops	x	H 1159	Military srvces	
–Skid resistance *(May Subd Geog)*	x	H 1158	Materials	
–Skidding *(May Subd Geog)*	x	H 1195	Land vehicles	
–Slang	x	H 1095	see *SCM:SH*	
		H 1154	Languages	
–Slavic influences	x	H 1156	Literatures	H 1675
–Slide collections	x	H 1105	Corp bodies	H 1427
		H 1110	Indiv pers	H 1427
		H 1120	Families	H 1427
–Slides	v	H 1095	see *SCM:SH*	
		H 1110	Indiv pers	
		H 1140	Places	
–Slovak influences	x	H 1156	Literatures	H 1675
–Small-boat service	x	H 1159	Military srvces	
–Snow protection and removal *(May Subd Geog)*	x	H 1195	Land vehicles	

SUBDIVISION	SUBFIELD CODE(S)	FREE-FLOATING LIST IN SCM:SH	CATEGORY	USAGE GUIDELINES IN SCM:SH
–Social aspects *(May Subd Geog)*	x	H 1095	see *SCM:SH*	
		H 1153	Industries	
		H 1154	Languages	
		H 1200	Wars	
–Social conditions	x	H 1100	Classes pers	H 2055
		H 1103	Ethnic groups	H 2055
		H 1140	Places	H 2055
		H 1149.5	Colonies	H 2055
–Social conditions–16th century	x–y	H 1100	Classes pers	H 2055
		H 1103	Ethnic grous	H 2055
		H 1140	Places	H 2055
–Social conditions–17th century	x–y	H 1100	Classes pers	H 2055
		H 1103	Ethnic grous	H 2055
		H 1140	Places	H 2055
–Social conditions–18th century	x–y	H 1100	Classes pers	H 2055
		H 1103	Ethnic grous	H 2055
		H 1140	Places	H 2055
–Social conditions–19th century	x–y	H 1100	Classes pers	H 2055
		H 1103	Ethnic grous	H 2055
		H 1140	Places	H 2055
–Social conditions–20th century	x–y	H 1100	Classes pers	H 2055
		H 1103	Ethnic grous	H 2055
		H 1140	Places	H 2055
–Social conditions–21st century	x–y	H 1100	Classes pers	H 2055
		H 1103	Ethnic grous	H 2055
		H 1140	Places	H 2055
–Social life and customs	x	H 1100	Classes pers	H 2057
		H 1103	Ethnic groups	H 2057
		H 1140	Places	H 2057
		H 1149.5	Colonies	H 2057
–Social life and customs–16th century	x–y	H 1100	Classes pers	H 2057
		H 1103	Ethnic grous	H 2057
		H 1140	Places	H 2057
–Social life and customs–17th century	x–y	H 1100	Classes pers	H 2057
		H 1103	Ethnic grous	H 2057
		H 1140	Places	H 2057

Free-floating Subdivisions: An Alphabetical Index

SUBDIVISION	SUBFIELD CODE(S)	FREE-FLOATING LIST IN SCM:SH	CATEGORY	USAGE GUIDELINES IN SCM:SH
–Social life and customs–18th century	x–y	H 1100 H 1103 H 1140	Classes pers Ethnic grous Places	H 2057 H 2057 H 2057
–Social life and customs–19th century	x–y	H 1100 H 1103 H 1140	Classes pers Ethnic grous Places	H 2057 H 2057 H 2057
–Social life and customs–20th century	x–y	H 1100 H 1103 H 1140	Classes pers Ethnic grous Places	H 2057 H 2057 H 2057
–Social life and customs–21st century	x–y	H 1100 H 1103 H 1140	Classes pers Ethnic grous Places	H 2057 H 2057 H 2057
–Social networks *(May Subd Geog)*	x	H 1100 H 1103	Classes pers Ethnic groups	
–Social policy	x	H 1140 H 1149.5	Places Colonies	
–Social scientific criticism *(May Subd Geog)*	x	H 1188	Sacred works	
–Social services	x	H 1159	Military srvces	
–Socialization *(May Subd Geog)*	x	H 1103	Ethnic groups	
–Societies and clubs	x	H 1100	Classes pers	H 2060
–Societies, etc.	x	H 1095 H 1100 H 1103 H 1105 H 1110 H 1188	see *SCM:SH* Classes pers Ethnic groups Corp bodies Indiv pers Sacred works	H 2060 H 2060 H 2060 H 2060 H 2060 H 2060
–Socio-rhetorical criticism *(May Subd Geog)*	x	H 1188	Sacred works	
–Sociological aspects	x	H 1095 H 1151.5	see *SCM:SH* Types schools	H 2055
–Software	v	H 1095	see *SCM:SH*	H 2070
–Soils *(May Subd Geog)*	x	H 1180	Plants & crops	

SUBDIVISION	SUBFIELD CODE(S)	FREE-FLOATING LIST IN SCM:SH	CATEGORY	USAGE GUIDELINES IN SCM:SH
–Solo with harpsichord	v	H 1160	Musical comps	
–Solo with harpsichord and piano	v	H 1160	Musical comps	
–Solo with keyboard instrument	v	H 1160	Musical comps	
–Solo with organ	v	H 1160	Musical comps	
–Solo with piano	v	H 1160	Musical comps	
–Solo with pianos (2)	v	H 1160	Musical comps	
–Solos with organ	v	H 1160	Musical comps	
–Solos with piano	v	H 1160	Musical comps	
–Solos with pianos (2)	v	H 1160	Musical comps	
–Solubility *(May Subd Geog)*	x	H 1149 H 1158	Chemicals Materials	
–Somatic embryogenesis *(May Subd Geog)*	x	H 1180	Plants & crops	
–Song-Yuan dynasties, 960-1368	y	H 1148	Chinese art	
–Songs and music	v	H 1095 H 1100 H 1103 H 1105 H 1110 H 1140 H 1159	see *SCM:SH* Classes pers Ethnic groups Corp bodies Indiv pers Places Military srvces	H 2075 H 2075 H 2075 H 2075 H 2075 H 2075 H 2075
–Songs and music–Discography	x–v	H 1095	see *SCM:SH*	
–Songs and music–History and criticism	x–x	H 1095	see *SCM:SH*	H 2075
–Songs and music–Texts	v–v	H 1095	see *SCM:SH*	H 2190
–Sonorants	x	H 1154	Languages	
–Sound recordings for foreign speakers	v	H 1154	Languages	
–Sound recordings for French, [Spanish, etc.] speakers	v	H 1154	Languages	

SUBDIVISION	SUBFIELD CODE(S)	FREE-FLOATING LIST IN SCM:SH	CATEGORY	USAGE GUIDELINES IN SCM:SH	
–Soundproofing *(May Subd Geog)*	x	H 1095	see *SCM:SH*		
–Sounds	x	H 1164	Organs of body		
		H 1200	Wars		
–Sources	x	H 1156	Literatures	H 2080	H 1647
–Sources	v	H 1095	see *SCM:SH*	H 2080	H 1647
		H 1110	Indiv pers	H 2080	H 1647
		H 1200	Wars	H 2080	H 1647
–South Asian authors	x	H 1156	Literatures		
–Soviet influences	x	H 1156	Literatures	H 1675	
–Sowing *(May Subd Geog)*	x	H 1180	Plants & crops		
–Spacing *(May Subd Geog)*	x	H 1180	Plants & crops		
–Spanish influences	x	H 1156	Literatures	H 1675	
–Spawning *(May Subd Geog)*	x	H 1147	Animals		
–Speakers	x	H 1155	Legis bodies		
–Speciation *(May Subd Geog)*	x	H 1147	Animals		
		H 1149	Chemicals		
		H 1180	Plants & crops		
–Specifications *(May Subd Geog)*	v	H 1095	see *SCM:SH*	H 2083	
		H 1153	Industries	H 2083	
		H 1158	Materials	H 2083	
–Specimens	v	H 1095	see *SCM:SH*		
–Spectra	x	H 1095	see *SCM:SH*		
		H 1149	Chemicals		
		H 1158	Materials		
–Spectral analysis	x	H 1154	Languages		
–Spectroscopic imaging *(May Subd Geog)*	x	H 1150	Diseases		
		H 1164	Organs of body		
–Speeches in Congress	v	H 1095	see *SCM:SH*		
–Speed	x	H 1195	Land vehicles		
		H 1147	Animals		

SUBDIVISION	SUBFIELD CODE(S)	FREE-FLOATING LIST IN SCM:SH	CATEGORY	USAGE GUIDELINES IN SCM:SH
–Spermatozoa	x	H 1147	Animals	
–Spermatozoa–Abnormalities *(May Subd Geog)*	x–x	H 1147	Animals	
–Spermatozoa–Morphology	x–x	H 1147	Animals	
–Spiritual life	x	H 1186	Relig orders	
–Spiritualistic interpretations	x	H 1110	Indiv pers	
–Spoken French, [Japanese, etc.] *(May Subd Geog)*	x	H 1154	Languages	
–Spores *(May Subd Geog)*	x	H 1180	Plants & crops	
–Spores–Morphology	x-x	H 1180	Plants & crops	
–Sports	x	H 1151 H 1159	Indiv schools Military srvces	
–Sports *(May Subd Geog)*	x	H 1103	Ethnic groups	
–Spray control *(May Subd Geog)*	x	H 1195	Land vehicles	
–Springs and suspension *(May Subd Geog)*	x	H 1195	Land vehicles	
–Spurious and doubtful works	v	H 1110	Indiv pers	
–Stability	x	H 1095 H 1149 H 1195	see *SCM:SH* Chemicals Land vehicles	
–Stability operations	x	H 1159	Military srvces	
–Staff corps	x	H 1159	Military srvces	
–Staffs	x	H 1159	Military srvces	
–Stage guides	v	H 1160	Musical comps	
–Stage history *(May Subd Geog)*	x	H 1110	Indiv pers	
–Stamp collections	x	H 1105 H 1110 H 1120	Corp bodies Indiv pers Families	H 1427 H 1427 H 1427

SUBDIVISION	SUBFIELD CODE(S)	FREE-FLOATING LIST IN SCM:SH	CATEGORY	USAGE GUIDELINES IN SCM:SH
–Standardization	x	H 1154	Languages	
–Standards *(May Subd Geog)*	x	H 1095	see *SCM:SH*	
		H 1149	Chemicals	
		H 1151.5	Types schools	
		H 1153	Industries	
–Starting devices *(May Subd Geog)*	x	H 1195	Land vehicles	
–State supervision *(May Subd Geog)*	x	H 1095	see *SCM:SH*	
		H 1153	Industries	
–States	x	H 1095	see *SCM:SH*	H 713
–Statistical methods	x	H 1095	see *SCM:SH*	H 2095
		H 1153	Industries	H 2095
–Statistical services	x	H 1095	see *SCM:SH*	H 2095
		H 1100	Classes pers	H 2095
		H 1103	Ethnic groups	H 2095
		H 1140	Places	H 2095
		H 1153	Industries	H 2095
–Statistical services–Law and legislation	x–x	H 1140	Places	
–Statistics	v	H 1095	see *SCM:SH*	H 2095
		H 1100	Classes pers	H 2095
		H 1103	Ethnic groups	H 2095
		H 1105	Corp bodies	H 2095
		H 1140	Places	H 2095
–Statistics, Medical	v	H 1140	Places	H 2095
–Statistics, Vital	v	H 1103	Ethnic groups	H 2095
		H 1140	Places	H 2095
–Statues *(May Subd Geog)*	x	H 1110	Indiv pers	
–Steering-gear	x	H 1195	Land vehicles	
–Stewards	x	H 1159	Military srvces	
–Storage *(May Subd Geog)*	x	H 1095	see *SCM:SH*	
		H 1180	Plants & crops	
–Storage–Climatic factors *(May Subd Geog)*	x–x	H 1180	Plants & crops	

SUBDIVISION	SUBFIELD CODE(S)	FREE-FLOATING LIST IN SCM:SH	CATEGORY	USAGE GUIDELINES IN SCM:SH
–Storage–Diseases and injuries (*May Subd Geog*)	x–x	H 1180	Plants & crops	
–Storekeepers	x	H 1159	Military srvces	
–Stories, plots, etc.	v	H 1110 H 1156 H 1160	Indiv pers Literatures Musical comps	
–Stranding (*May Subd Geog*)	x	H 1147	Animals	
–Strategic aspects	x	H 1140	Places	
–Stress corrosion (*May Subd Geog*)	x	H 1158	Materials	
–Structuralist criticism (*May Subd Geog*)	x	H 1188	Sacred works	
–Structure	x	H 1149	Chemicals	
–Structure-activity relationships	x	H 1149	Chemicals	
–Student housing	x	H 1151	Indiv schools	
–Student strike, [date]	x	H 1151	Indiv schools	
–Students	x	H 1151	Indiv schools	
–Students–Yearbooks	x–v	H 1151	Indiv schools	H 2400
–Studies and exercises	v	H 1161	Musical instrum	
–Studies and exercises–Juvenile	v–v	H 1161	Musical instrum	
–Studies and exercises (Alternative rock)	v	H 1161	Musical instrum	
–Studies and exercises (Big band)	v	H 1161	Musical instrum	
–Studies and exercises (Bluegrass)	v	H 1161	Musical instrum	
–Studies and exercises (Blues)	v	H 1161	Musical instrum	
–Studies and exercises (Blues-rock)	v	H 1161	Musical instrum	
–Studies and exercises (Boogie woogie)	v	H 1161	Musical instrum	

SUBDIVISION	SUBFIELD CODE(S)	FREE-FLOATING LIST IN SCM:SH	CATEGORY	USAGE GUIDELINES IN SCM:SH
–Studies and exercises (Bop)	v	H 1161	Musical instrum	
–Studies and exercises (Celtic)	v	H 1161	Musical instrum	
–Studies and exercises (Country)	v	H 1161	Musical instrum	
–Studies and exercises (Dixieland)	v	H 1161	Musical instrum	
–Studies and exercises (Folk)	v	H 1161	Musical instrum	
–Studies and exercises (Funk)	v	H 1161	Musical instrum	
–Studies and exercises (Gospel)	v	H 1161	Musical instrum	
–Studies and exercises (Heavy metal)	v	H 1161	Musical instrum	
–Studies and exercises (Honky-tonk)	v	H 1161	Musical instrum	
–Studies and exercises (Jazz)	v	H 1161	Musical instrum	
–Studies and exercises (Jazz-rock)	v	H 1161	Musical instrum	
–Studies and exercises (Latin jazz)	v	H 1161	Musical instrum	
–Studies and exercises (Left hand)	v	H 1161	Musical instrum	
–Studies and exercises (Popular music)	v	H 1161	Musical instrum	
–Studies and exercises (Progressive rock)	v	H 1161	Musical instrum	
–Studies and exercises (Ragtime)	v	H 1161	Musical instrum	
–Studies and exercises (Reggae)	v	H 1161	Musical instrum	
–Studies and exercises (Rhythm and blues)	v	H 1161	Musical instrum	
–Studies and exercises (Right hand)	v	H 1161	Musical instrum	
–Studies and exercises (Rock)	v	H 1161	Musical instrum	
–Studies and exercises (Swing)	v	H 1161	Musical instrum	
–Studies and exercises (Western swing)	v	H 1161	Musical instrum	

SUBDIVISION	SUBFIELD CODE(S)	FREE-FLOATING LIST IN SCM:SH	CATEGORY	USAGE GUIDELINES IN SCM:SH
–Study and teaching *(May Subd Geog)*	x	H 1095	see *SCM:SH*	H 2110
		H 1100	Classes pers	H 2110
		H 1103	Ethnic groups	H 2110
		H 1140	Places	H 2110
		H 1154	Languages	H 2110
		H 1188	Sacred works	H 2110
–Study and teaching–Activity programs *(May Subd Geog)*	x–x	H 1095	see *SCM:SH*	
–Study and teaching–African American students	x–x	H 1154	Languages	
–Study and teaching–Audio-visual aids	x–x	H 1095	see *SCM:SH*	H 2110
–Study and teaching–Baptists, [Catholic Church, etc.]	x–x	H 1188	Sacred works	
–Study and teaching–Bilingual method	x–x	H 1154	Languages	
–Study and teaching–Foreign speakers	x–x	H 1154	Languages	
–Study and teaching–Foreign speakers–Audio-visual aids	x–x–x	H 1154	Languages	
–Study and teaching–French, [Spanish, etc.] speakers	x–x	H 1154	Languages	
–Study and teaching–Immersion method	x–x	H 1154	Languages	
–Study and teaching–Law and legislation *(May Subd Geog)*	x–x	H 1140	Places	
–Study and teaching–Simulation methods	x–x	H 1095	see *SCM:SH*	H 2110
–Study and teaching–Supervision *(May Subd Geog)*	x–x	H 1095	see *SCM:SH*	
–Study and teaching (Continuing education) *(May Subd Geog)*	x	H 1095	see *SCM:SH*	H 2110
		H 1154	Languages	H 2110
–Study and teaching (Continuing education)–Audio-visual aids	x–x	H 1095	see *SCM:SH*	

SUBDIVISION	SUBFIELD CODE(S)	FREE-FLOATING LIST IN SCM:SH	CATEGORY	USAGE GUIDELINES IN SCM:SH
–Study and teaching (Continuing education)–Foreign speakers	x–x	H 1154	Languages	
–Study and teaching (Continuing education)–French, [Spanish, etc.] speakers	x–x	H 1154	Languages	
–Study and teaching (Early childhood) *(May Subd Geog)*	x	H 1095 H 1154	see *SCM:SH* Languages	H 2110
–Study and teaching (Early childhood)–Activity programs *(May Subd Geog)*	x–x	H 1095	see *SCM:SH*	
–Study and teaching (Early childhood)–Audio-visual aids	x–x	H 1095	see *SCM:SH*	
–Study and teaching (Early childhood)–Foreign speakers	x–x	H 1154	Languages	
–Study and teaching (Early childhood)–French, [Spanish etc.] speakers	x–x	H 1154	Languages	
–Study and teaching (Elementary) *(May Subd Geog)*	x	H 1095 H 1154	see *SCM:SH* Languages	H 2110 H 2110
–Study and teaching (Elementary)–Activity programs *(May Subd Geog)*	x–x	H 1095	see *SCM:SH*	
–Study and teaching (Elementary)–Audio-visual aids	x–x	H 1095	see *SCM:SH*	
–Study and teaching (Elementary)–Foreign speakers	x–x	H 1154	Languages	
–Study and teaching (Elementary)–French, [Spanish, etc.] speakers	x–x	H 1154	Languages	
–Study and teaching (Elementary)–Simulation methods	x–x	H 1095	see *SCM:SH*	
–Study and teaching (Graduate) *(May Subd Geog)*	x	H 1095	see *SCM:SH*	H 2110
–Study and teaching (Higher) *(May Subd Geog)*	x	H 1095 H 1154	see *SCM:SH* Languages	H 2110 H 2110

SUBDIVISION	SUBFIELD CODE(S)	FREE-FLOATING LIST IN SCM:SH	CATEGORY	USAGE GUIDELINES IN SCM:SH
–Study and teaching (Higher)–Activity programs *(May Subd Geog)*	x–x	H 1095	see *SCM:SH*	
–Study and teaching (Higher)–Audio-visual aids	x–x	H 1095	see *SCM:SH*	
–Study and teaching (Higher)–Foreign speakers	x–x	H 1154	Languages	
–Study and teaching (Higher)–French, [Spanish, etc.] speakers	x–x	H 1154	Languages	
–Study and teaching (Higher)–Simulation methods	x–x	H 1095	see *SCM:SH*	
–Study and teaching (Internship) *(May Subd Geog)*	x	H 1095 H 1103 H 1105 H 1140	see *SCM:SH* Ethnic groups Corp bodies Places	H 2110 H 2110 H 2110 H 2110
–Study and teaching (Middle school *(May Subd Geog)*	x	H 1095	see *SCM:SH*	H 2110
–Study and teaching (Middle school)–Activity programs *(May Subd Geog)*	x–x	H 1095	see *SCM:SH*	
–Study and teaching (Middle school)–Audio-visual aids	x–x	H 1095	see *SCM:SH*	
–Study and teaching (Preschool) *(May Subd Geog)*	x	H 1095 H 1154	see *SCM:SH* Languages	H 2110
–Study and teaching (Preschool)–Activity programs *(May Subd Geog)*	x–x	H 1095	see *SCM:SH*	
–Study and teaching (Preschool)–Audio-visual aids	x–x	H 1095	see *SCM:SH*	
–Study and teaching (Preschool)–Foreign speakers	x–x	H 1154	Languages	
–Study and teaching (Preschool)–French, [Spanish, etc.] speakers	x–x	H 1154	Languages	

SUBDIVISION	SUBFIELD CODE(S)	FREE-FLOATING LIST IN SCM:SH	CATEGORY	USAGE GUIDELINES IN SCM:SH
–Study and teaching (Primary) *(May Subd Geog)*	x	H 1095 H 1154	see *SCM:SH* Languages	H 2110 H 2110
–Study and teaching (Primary)– Activity programs *(May Subd Geog)*	x–x	H 1095	see *SCM:SH*	
–Study and teaching (Primary)– Audio-visual aids	x–x	H 1095	see *SCM:SH*	
–Study and teaching (Primary)– Foreign speakers	x–x	H 1154	Languages	
–Study and teaching (Primary)– French, [Spanish, etc.] speakers	x–x	H 1154	Languages	H 2110
–Study and teaching (Residency) *(May Subd Geog)*	x	H 1095	see *SCM:SH*	H 2110
–Study and teaching (Secondary) *(May Subd Geog)*	x	H 1095 H 1154	see *SCM:SH* Languages	H 2110 H 2110
–Study and teaching (Secondary)– Activity programs *(May Subd Geog)*	x–x	H 1095	see *SCM:SH*	
–Study and teaching (Secondary)– Audio-visual aids	x–x	H 1095	see *SCM:SH*	
–Study and teaching (Secondary)– Foreign speakers	x–x	H 1154	Languages	
–Study and teaching (Secondary)– French, [Spanish, etc.] speakers	x–x	H 1154	Languages	
–Study and teaching (Secondary)– Simulation methods	x–x	H 1095	see *SCM:SH*	
–Study guides	v	H 1095	see *SCM:SH*	
–Style	x	H 1154 H 1155.8	Languages Lit works/Title	
–Subcontracting *(May Subd Geog)*	x	H 1153	Industries	
–Subjectless constructions	x	H 1154	Languages	
–Subjunctive	x	H 1154	Languages	

SUBDIVISION	SUBFIELD CODE(S)	FREE-FLOATING LIST IN SCM:SH	CATEGORY	USAGE GUIDELINES IN SCM:SH
–Submarine forces	x	H 1159	Military srvces	
–Subordinate constructions	x	H 1154	Languages	
–Subsidies *(May Subd Geog)*	x	H 1153	Industries	
–Substance use *(May Subd Geog)*	x	H 1100 H 1103	Classes pers Ethnic groups	
–Substitution	x	H 1154	Languages	
–Suffixes and prefixes	x	H 1154	Languages	
–Suffrage *(May Subd Geog)*	x	H 1100 H 1103	Classes pers Ethnic groups	
–Suicidal behavior *(May Subd Geog)*	x	H 1100 H 1103	Classes pers Ethnic groups	
–Summering *(May Subd Geog)*	x	H 1147	Animals	
–Supervision of *(May Subd Geog)*	x	H 1100	Classes pers	
–Supplementary employment *(May Subd Geog)*	x	H 1100 H 1103	Classes pers Ethnic groups	
–Suppletion	x	H 1154	Languages	
–Supplies and stores	x	H 1159	Military srvces	
–Supplies and stores–Law and legislation	x–x	H 1159	Military srvces	
–Supplies and stores–Quality control	x–x	H 1159	Military srvces	
–Supply and demand *(May Subd Geog)*	x	H 1100	Classes pers	
–Surfaces	x	H 1149 H 1158	Chemicals Materials	
–Surfaces–Defects *(May Subd Geog)*	x–x	H 1158	Materials	
–Surfaces–Optical properties	x–x	H 1158	Materials	
–Surgeons	x	H 1159	Military srvces	

SUBDIVISION	SUBFIELD CODE(S)	FREE-FLOATING LIST IN SCM:SH	CATEGORY	USAGE GUIDELINES IN SCM:SH
–Surgeons–Malpractice	x–x	H 1159	Military srvces	
–Surgery *(May Subd Geog)*	x	H 1100	Classes pers	
		H 1103	Ethnic groups	
		H 1147	Animals	
		H 1150	Diseases	
		H 1164	Organs of body	
–Surgery–Complications *(May Subd Geog)*	x–x	H 1100	Classes pers	
		H 1147	Animals	
		H 1150	Diseases	
		H 1164	Organs of body	
–Surgery–Instruments	x–x	H 1164	Organs of body	
–Surgery–Instruments– Sterilization *(May Subd Geog)*	x–x–x	H 1164	Organs of body	
–Surgery–Nursing *(May Subd Geog)*	x–x	H 1147	Animals	
		H 1150	Diseases	
		H 1164	Organs of body	
–Surgery–Nutritional aspects *(May Subd Geog)*	x–x	H 1164	Organs of body	
–Surgery–Patients *(May Subd Geog)*	x–x	H 1164	Organs of body	
–Surgery–Risk factors *(May Subd Geog)*	x–x	H 1100	Classes pers	
		H 1164	Organs of body	
–Surveys	v	H 1140	Places	
–Susceptibility *(May Subd Geog)*	x	H 1150	Diseases	
–Suspension *(May Subd Geog)*	x	H 1100	Classes pers	
–Swami-Narayani authors	x	H 1156	Literatures	
–Swimming	x	H 1151	Indiv schools	
–Swiss Americans	x	H 1159	Military srvces	
–Switch-reference	x	H 1154	Languages	
–Syllabication	x	H 1154	Languages	
–Symbolic aspects *(May Subd Geog)*	x	H 1147	Animals	
		H 1164	Organs of body	

SUBDIVISION	SUBFIELD CODE(S)	FREE-FLOATING LIST IN SCM:SH	CATEGORY	USAGE GUIDELINES IN SCM:SH
–Symbolic representation	x	H 1140	Places	
–Symbolism	x	H 1110	Indiv pers	
–Synonyms and antonyms	x	H 1154	Languages	
–Syntax	x	H 1154	Languages	
–Synthesis	x	H 1149	Chemicals	
–Synthesis–Inhibitors	x–x	H 1149	Chemicals	
–Synthesis–Regulation	x–x	H 1149	Chemicals	
–Syphilis *(May Subd Geog)*	x	H 1164	Organs of body	
–Tables	v	H 1095	see *SCM:SH*	H 2160
–Tables of contents	v	H 1095	see *SCM:SH*	
–Tactical aviation *(May Subd Geog)*	x	H 1159	Military srvces	
–Taishō period, 1912-1926	y	H 1148	Japanese art	
–Tang-Five dynasties, 618-960	y	H 1148	Chinese art	
–Tank warfare	x	H 1200	Wars	
–Taoist influences	x	H 1156	Literatures	H 1675
–Target practice	x	H 1159	Military srvces	
–Taxation *(May Subd Geog)*	x	H 1095 H 1100 H 1103	see *SCM:SH* Classes pers Ethnic groups	
–Taxation–Law and legislation *(May Subd Geog)*	x–x	H 1095 H 1100 H 1103	see *SCM:SH* Classes pers Ethnic groups	
–Teaching office	x	H 1187	Christian denom	
–Teaching pieces	v	H 1160	Musical comps	
–Teachings	x	H 1110	Indiv pers	

SUBDIVISION	SUBFIELD CODE(S)	FREE-FLOATING LIST IN SCM:SH	CATEGORY	USAGE GUIDELINES IN SCM:SH
–Technique	x	H 1095 H 1110 H 1148	see *SCM:SH* Indiv pers Art	
–Technological innovations *(May Subd Geog)*	x	H 1095 H 1147 H 1153 H 1180	see *SCM:SH* Animals Industries Plants & crops	
–Technology	x	H 1200	Wars	
–Teenagers' use *(May Subd Geog)*	x	H 1188	Sacred works	
–Telephone directories	v	H 1095 H 1100 H 1103 H 1105 H 1140 H 1153	see *SCM:SH* Classes pers Ethnic groups Corp bodies Places Industries	H 1558 H 1558 H 1558 H 1558 H 1558 H 1558
–Telephone directories–Yellow pages	v–v	H 1140	Places	
–Television and the war, [revolution, etc.]	x	H 1200	Wars	
–Television broadcasting of proceedings	x	H 1155	Legis bodies	
–Temperature *(May Subd Geog)*	x	H 1180	Plants & crops	
–Tempo	x	H 1154	Languages	
–Temporal clauses	x	H 1154	Languages	
–Temporal constructions	x	H 1154	Languages	
–Tennis	x	H 1151	Indiv schools	
–Tense	x	H 1154	Languages	
–Term of office	x	H 1155	Legis bodies	
–Terminology	v	H 1095 H 1100 H 1105 H 1188	see *SCM:SH* Classes pers Corp bodies Sacred works	H 2184 H 2184 H 2184 H 2184

SUBDIVISION	SUBFIELD CODE(S)	FREE-FLOATING LIST IN SCM:SH	CATEGORY	USAGE GUIDELINES IN SCM:SH	
–Terminology–Pronunciation	x–x	H 1095 H 1188	see *SCM:SH* Sacred works		
–Terms and phrases	v	H 1154	Languages	H 1540	H 2184
–Territorial expansion	x	H 1140	Places		
–Territorial questions *(May Subd Geog)*	x	H 1200	Wars	H 1333.5	
–Territoriality *(May Subd Geog)*	x	H 1147	Animals		
–Territories and possessions	x	H 1095 H 1140	see *SCM:SH* Places	H 2185 H 2185	
–Territories and possessions–Politics and government	x–x	H 1140	Places		
–Test shooting	x	H 1159	Military srvces		
–Testing	x	H 1095 H 1147 H 1149 H 1158	see *SCM:SH* Animals Chemicals Materials	H 2186 H 2186 H 2186 H 2186	
–Textbooks	v	H 1095 H 1154 H 1188	see *SCM:SH* Languages Sacred works	H 2187 H 2187 H 2187	H 1690 H 1690 H 1690
–Textbooks for English, [French, etc.] speakers	v	H 1154	Languages	H 2187	
–Textbooks for foreign speakers	v	H 1154	Languages	H 2187	
–Textbooks for foreign speakers–English	v–x	H 1154	Languages	H 2187	
–Textbooks for foreign speakers–German, [Italian, etc.]	v–x	H 1154	Languages	H 2187	
–Texts	v	H 1095 H 1154 H 1160	see *SCM:SH* Languages Musical comps	H 2190 H 2190 H 2190	
–Texts–Dating	x–x	H 1154	Languages		
–Texture *(May Subd Geog)*	x	H 1158	Materials		

SUBDIVISION	SUBFIELD CODE(S)	FREE-FLOATING LIST IN SCM:SH	CATEGORY	USAGE GUIDELINES IN SCM:SH
–Theater and the war, [revolution, etc.]	x	H 1200	Wars	
–Thematic catalogs	v	H 1110 H 1160	Indiv pers Musical comps	
–Themes, motives	x	H 1095 H 1110 H 1148 H 1156	see *SCM:SH* Indiv pers Art Literatures	
–Theology	x	H 1186 H 1188	Relig orders Sacred works	H 1295
–Therapeutic use *(May Subd Geog)*	x	H 1095 H 1147 H 1149 H 1180	see *SCM:SH* Animals Chemicals Plants & crops	
–Therapeutic use–Administration	x–x	H 1149	Chemicals	
–Therapeutic use–Controlled release *(May Subd Geog)*	x–x	H 1149	Chemicals	
–Therapeutic use–Effectiveness *(May Subd Geog)*	x–x	H 1149	Chemicals	
–Therapeutic use–Side effects *(May Subd Geog)*	x–x	H 1149 H 1180	Chemicals Plants & crops	
–Therapeutic use–Testing	x–x	H 1149	Chemicals	
–Thermal conductivity *(May Subd Geog)*	x	H 1149 H 1158	Chemicals Materials	
–Thermal fatigue *(May Subd Geog)*	x	H 1158	Materials	
–Thermal properties *(May Subd Geog)*	x	H 1149 H 1158 H 1180	Chemicals Materials Plants & crops	
–Thermography *(May Subd Geog)*	x	H 1164	Organs of body	
–Thermomechanical properties	x	H 1158	Materials	
–Thermomechanical treatment *(May Subd Geog)*	x	H 1158	Materials	

SUBDIVISION	SUBFIELD CODE(S)	FREE-FLOATING LIST IN SCM:SH	CATEGORY	USAGE GUIDELINES IN SCM:SH
–Thermotherapy *(May Subd Geog)*	x	H 1150	Diseases	
–Thinning *(May Subd Geog)*	x	H 1180	Plants & crops	
–Three kingdoms-Sui dynasty, 220-618	y	H 1148	Chinese art	
–Threshing *(May Subd Geog)*	x	H 1180	Plants & crops	
–Threshing–Machinery *(May Subd Geog)*	x	H 1180	Plants & crops	
–Threshold limit values *(May Subd Geog)*	x	H 1149	Chemicals	
–Time management *(May Subd Geog)*	x	H 1100 H 1103	Classes pers Ethnic groups	
–Tires	x	H 1195	Land vehicles	
–Tires–Inflation pressure	x–x	H 1195	Land vehicles	
–Tires–Repairing *(May Subd Geog)*	x–x	H 1195	Land vehicles	
–Titles	x	H 1100 H 1110	Classes pers Indiv pers	
–Titles of books	x	H 1188	Sacred works	
–To 221 B.C.	y	H 1148	Chinese art	
–To 500	y	H 1160	Musical comps	
–To 794	y	H 1148	Japanese art	
–To 935	y	H 1148	Korean art	
–To 1500	y	H 1156	Drama	
–To 1600	y	H 1148	Japanese art	
–To 1868	y	H 1148	Japanese art	
–To 1900	y	H 1148	Korean art	
–Tobacco use *(May Subd Geog)*	x	H 1100 H 1103	Classes pers Ethnic groups	

SUBDIVISION	SUBFIELD CODE(S)	FREE-FLOATING LIST IN SCM:SH	CATEGORY	USAGE GUIDELINES IN SCM:SH
–Tomb	x	H 1110	Indiv pers	
–Tombs *(May Subd Geog)*	x	H 1095	see *SCM:SH*	
		H 1100	Classes pers	
		H 1120	Families	
–Tomography *(May Subd Geog)*	x	H 1150	Diseases	
		H 1164	Organs of body	
–Tonguing	x	H 1161	Musical instrum	
–Topic and comment	x	H 1154	Languages	
–Tours	v	H 1105	Corp bodies	H 1530
		H 1140	Places	H 1530
–Towing *(May Subd Geog)*	x	H 1195	Land vehicles	
–Toxicity testing *(May Subd Geog)*	x	H 1149	Chemicals	
–Toxicology *(May Subd Geog)*	x	H 1095	see *SCM:SH*	
		H 1147	Animals	
		H 1149	Chemicals	
		H 1158	Materials	
		H 1180	Plants & crops	
–Toxicology–Age factors *(May Subd Geog)*	x–x	H 1149	Chemicals	
–Toxicology–Biography	x–v	H 1149	Chemicals	
–Toxicology–Reporting *(May Subd Geog)*	x–x	H 1149	Chemicals	
–Track and field	x	H 1151	Indiv schools	
–Traction *(May Subd Geog)*	x	H 1164	Organs of body	
		H 1195	Land vehicles	
–Trademarks	v	H 1095	see *SCM:SH*	
		H 1153	Industries	
–Tragedies	x	H 1110	Indiv pers	
–Tragicomedies	x	H 1110	Indiv pers	
–Training *(May Subd Geog)*	x	H 1147	Animals	
		H 1180	Plants & crops	

SUBDIVISION	SUBFIELD CODE(S)	FREE-FLOATING LIST IN SCM:SH	CATEGORY	USAGE GUIDELINES IN SCM:SH	
–Training administrators	x	H 1159	Military srvces		
–Training of *(May Subd Geog)*	x	H 1100	Classes pers	H 2217	H 2110
–Transaxles	x	H 1195	Land vehicles		
–Transcription *(May Subd Geog)*	x	H 1154	Languages		
–Transfer	x	H 1100	Classes pers		
–Transition periods	x	H 1155	Legis bodies		
–Transitivity	x	H 1154	Languages		
–Translating *(May Subd Geog)*	x	H 1095	see *SCM:SH*	H 2219	
		H 1154	Languages	H 2219	
		H 1188	Sacred works	H 2219	
–Translating into French, [German, etc.]	x	H 1154	Languages	H 2219	
–Translations	v	H 1095	see *SCM:SH*	H 2220	
		H 1110	Indiv pers	H 2220	
		H 1155.8	Lit works/Title	H 2220	
		H 1156	Literatures	H 2220	
–Translations–History and criticism	x–x	H 1110	Indiv pers	H 2220	
		H 1155.8	Lit works/Title	H 2220	
		H 1156	Literatures	H 2220	
–Translations into French, [German, etc.]	v	H 1095	see *SCM:SH*		
		H 1110	Indiv pers	H 2220	
		H 1155.8	Lit works/Title	H 2220	
		H 1156	Literatures		
–Translations into French, [German, etc.]–History and criticism	x–x	H 1110	Indiv pers	H 2220	
		H 1155.8	Lit works/Title	H 2220	
		H 1156	Literatures		
–Transliteration	x	H 1154	Languages		
–Transliteration into Korean, [Russian, etc.]	x	H 1154	Languages		
–Transmission *(May Subd Geog)*	x	H 1150	Diseases		
–Transmission devices	x	H 1195	Land vehicles		

SUBDIVISION	SUBFIELD CODE(S)	FREE-FLOATING LIST IN SCM:SH	CATEGORY	USAGE GUIDELINES IN SCM:SH
–Transmission devices, Automatic	x	H 1195	Land vehicles	
–Transmission devices, Automatic– Parts *(May Subd Geog)*	x–x	H 1195	Land vehicles	
–Transmutation	x	H 1154	Languages	
–Transplantation *(May Subd Geog)*	x	H 1164	Organs of body	
–Transplantation–Complications *(May Subd Geog)*	x–x	H 1164	Organs of body	
–Transplantation–Immunological aspects	x–x	H 1164	Organs of body	
–Transplantation–Law and legislation *(May Subd Geog)*	x–x	H 1164	Organs of body	
–Transplantation–Nursing *(May Subd Geog)*	x–x	H 1164	Organs of body	
–Transplantation–Patients *(May Subd Geog)*	x–x	H 1164	Organs of body	
–Transplanting *(May Subd Geog)*	x	H 1180	Plants & crops	
–Transplanting–Machinery *(May Subd Geog)*	x–x	H 1180	Plants & crops	
–Transport of sick and wounded	x	H 1159	Military srvces	
–Transport properties *(May Subd Geog)*	x	H 1149 H 1158	Chemicals Materials	
–Transport service	x	H 1159	Military srvces	
–Transportation	x	H 1159	Military srvces	H 2225
–Transportation *(May Subd Geog)*	x	H 1095 H 1100 H 1103 H 1147 H 1158 H 1159 H 1180 H 1195 H 1200	see *SCM:SH* Classes pers Ethnic groups Animals Materials Military srvces Plants & crops Land vehicles Wars	H 2225 H 2225 H 2225 H 2225 H 2225 H 2225 H 2225 H 2225 H 2225

SUBDIVISION	SUBFIELD CODE(S)	FREE-FLOATING LIST IN SCM:SH	CATEGORY	USAGE GUIDELINES IN SCM:SH
–Transportation–Diseases and injuries *(May Subd Geog)*	x–x	H 1180	Plants & crops	
–Transportation–Law and legislation *(May Subd Geog)*	x–x	H 1158 H 1195	Materials Land vehicles	
–Trapping *(May Subd Geog)*	x	H 1103	Ethnic groups	
–Travel *(May Subd Geog)*	x	H 1100 H 1103 H 1105 H 1110	Classes pers Ethnic groups Corp bodies Indiv pers	
–Treaties	v	H 1103 H 1200	Ethnic groups Wars	H 2227 H 2227
–Treatment *(May Subd Geog)*	x	H 1150	Diseases	
–Treatment–Complications *(May Subd Geog)*	x–x	H 1150	Diseases	
–Trench warfare	x	H 1200	Wars	
–Trial practice	x	H 1154.5	Legal topics	
–Trials, litigation, etc.	v	H 1105 H 1110 H 1120 H 1140	Corp bodies Indiv pers Families Places	H 2228 H 2228 H 2228 H 2228
–Trials of vessels	x	H 1159	Military srvces	
–Tribal citizenship *(May Subd Geog)*	x	H 1103	Ethnic groups	
–Tritium content *(May Subd Geog)*	x	H 1158	Materials	
–Trophies	x	H 1200	Wars	
–Tropical conditions	x	H 1095	see *SCM:SH*	
–Trypanotolerance *(May Subd Geog)*	x	H 1147	Animals	
–Tuberculosis *(May Subd Geog)*	x	H 1164	Organs of body	
–Tuition	x	H 1151	Indiv schools	
–Tumors *(May Subd Geog)*	x	H 1164	Organs of body	

SUBDIVISION	SUBFIELD CODE(S)	FREE-FLOATING LIST IN SCM:SH	CATEGORY	USAGE GUIDELINES IN SCM:SH
–Tuning *(May Subd Geog)*	x	H 1161	Musical instrum	
–Tunnel warfare *(May Subd Geog)*	x	H 1200	Wars	
–Turkic influences	x	H 1156	Literatures	H 1675
–Turkish authors	x	H 1156	Literatures	
–Type specimens *(May Subd Geog)*	x	H 1147 H 1180	Animals Plants & crops	
–Ukrainian authors	x	H 1156	Literatures	
–Ukrainian influences	x	H 1156	Literatures	H 1675
–Ulcers *(May Subd Geog)*	x	H 1164	Organs of body	
–Ultrasonic imaging *(May Subd Geog)*	x	H 1150 H 1164	Diseases Organs of body	
–Ultrastructure	x	H 1164 H 1180	Organs of body Plants & crops	
–Undergraduates	x	H 1151	Indiv schools	
–Underground literature *(May Subd Geog)*	x	H 1200	Wars	
–Underground movements *(May Subd Geog)*	x	H 1200	Wars	
–Underground printing plants *(May Subd Geog)*	x	H 1200	Wars	
–Uniforms	x	H 1100 H 1105 H 1159	Classes pers Corp bodies Military srvces	
–Union lists	v	H 1095	see *SCM:SH*	H 1361
–Union territories	x	H 1095	see *SCM:SH*	H 713
–Unit cohesion	x	H 1159	Military srvces	
–Unknown military personnel	x	H 1200	Wars	
–Unknown military personnel, American, [British, etc.]	x	H 1200	Wars	

SUBDIVISION	SUBFIELD CODE(S)	FREE-FLOATING LIST IN SCM:SH	CATEGORY	USAGE GUIDELINES IN SCM:SH
–Upholstery *(May Subd Geog)*	x	H 1195	Land vehicles	
–Urdu influences	x	H 1156	Literatures	H 1675
–Usage	x	H 1154	Languages	
–Use	x	H 1188	Sacred works	
–Use studies	v	H 1095	see *SCM:SH*	
–Use in hymns	x	H 1188	Sacred works	
–Utilization *(May Subd Geog)*	x	H 1180	Plants & crops	
–Vaccination *(May Subd Geog)*	x	H 1150	Diseases	
		H 1147	Animals	
–Vaccination–Complications *(May Subd Geog)*	x–x	H 1150	Diseases	
–Validity *(May Subd Geog)*	x	H 1095	see *SCM:SH*	
–Valuation *(May Subd Geog)*	x	H 1095	see *SCM:SH*	
–Vapor pressure *(May Subd Geog)*	x	H 1149	Chemicals	
–Variation *(May Subd Geog)*	x	H 1147	Animals	
		H 1154	Languages	
		H 1164	Organs of body	
		H 1180	Plants & crops	
–Varieties *(May Subd Geog)*	x	H 1180	Plants & crops	
–Vegetative propagation *(May Subd Geog)*	x	H 1180	Plants & crops	
–Venom *(May Subd Geog)*	x	H 1147	Animals	
–Venom resistance *(May Subd Geog)*	x	H 1147	Animals	
–Verb	x	H 1154	Languages	
–Verb phrase	x	H 1154	Languages	
–Verbals	x	H 1154	Languages	

SUBDIVISION	SUBFIELD CODE(S)	FREE-FLOATING LIST IN SCM:SH	CATEGORY	USAGE GUIDELINES IN SCM:SH
–Versification	x	H 1110 H 1154 H 1155.8	Indiv pers Languages Lit works/Title	
–Versions	x	H 1188	Sacred works	H 1300
–Versions–Authorized, [Living Bible, Revised Standard, etc.]	x–x	H 1188	Sacred works	H 1300
–Versions, African, [Indic, Slavic, etc.]	x	H 1188	Sacred works	H 1300
–Versions, Baptist	x	H 1188	Sacred works	H 1300
–Versions, Catholic	x	H 1188	Sacred works	H 1300
–Versions, Catholic vs. Protestant	x	H 1188	Sacred works	H 1300
–Versions, Hussite	x	H 1188	Sacred works	H 1300
–Versions, Jehovah's Witnesses	x	H 1188	Sacred works	H 1300
–Vertical distribution *(May Subd Geog)*	x	H 1147	Animals	
–Vertical integration *(May Subd Geog)*	x	H 1153	Industries	
–Veterans *(May Subd Geog)*	x	H 1200	Wars	
–Veterinary service *(May Subd Geog)*	x	H 1200	Wars	
–Vibration *(May Subd Geog)*	x	H 1095 H 1195	see *SCM:SH* Land vehicles	
–Video catalogs	v	H 1095	see *SCM:SH*	H 1361
–Video recordings for foreign speakers	v	H 1154	Languages	
–Video recordings for French, [Spanish, etc.] speakers	v	H 1154	Languages	
–Violence against *(May Subd Geog)*	x	H 1100 H 1103	Classes pers Ethnic groups	
–Virus diseases *(May Subd Geog)*	x	H 1147	Animals	

SUBDIVISION	SUBFIELD CODE(S)	FREE-FLOATING LIST IN SCM:SH	CATEGORY	USAGE GUIDELINES IN SCM:SH
–Viruses *(May Subd Geog)*	x	H 1147	Animals	
–Viscosity *(May Subd Geog)*	x	H 1149 H 1158	Chemicals Materials	
–Vitality *(May Subd Geog)*	x	H 1180	Plants & crops	
–Vocabulary	x	H 1154	Languages	
–Vocal scores with accordion	v	H 1160	Musical comps	
–Vocal scores with continuo	v	H 1160	Musical comps	
–Vocal scores with guitar	v	H 1160	Musical comps	
–Vocal scores with harp	v	H 1160	Musical comps	
–Vocal scores with harpsichord	v	H 1160	Musical comps	
–Vocal scores with keyboard instrument	v	H 1160	Musical comps	
–Vocal scores with organ	v	H 1160	Musical comps	
–Vocal scores with organ and piano	v	H 1160	Musical comps	
–Vocal scores with piano	v	H 1160	Musical comps	
–Vocal scores with piano (4 hands)	v	H 1160	Musical comps	
–Vocal scores with pianos (2)	v	H 1160	Musical comps	
–Vocal scores without accompaniment	v	H 1160	Musical comps	
–Vocalization	x	H 1154	Languages	
–Vocalization *(May Subd Geog)*	x	H 1147	Animals	
–Vocalization–Regulation	x–x	H 1147	Animals	
–Vocational guidance *(May Subd Geog)*	x	H 1095 H 1100 H 1105 H 1153 H 1154 H 1159	see *SCM:SH* Classes pers Corp bodies Industries Languages Military srvces	H 2232 H 2232 H 2232 H 2232 H 2232 H 2232

SUBDIVISION	SUBFIELD CODE(S)	FREE-FLOATING LIST IN SCM:SH	CATEGORY	USAGE GUIDELINES IN SCM:SH
–Voice	x	H 1154	Languages	
–Voivodeships	x	H 1095	see *SCM:SH*	
–Volleyball	x	H 1151	Indiv schools	
–Voting	x	H 1155	Legis bodies	
–Vowel gradation	x	H 1154	Languages	
–Vowel reduction	x	H 1154	Languages	
–Vowels	x	H 1154	Languages	
–Wage fixing	x	H 1159	Military srvces	
–War use *(May Subd Geog)*	x	H 1158	Materials	
–War work *(May Subd Geog)*	x	H 1200	Wars	
–War work–American Legion	x–x	H 1200	Wars	
–War work–Boy Scouts	x–x	H 1200	Wars	
–War work–Catholic Church, [Methodist Church, etc.]	x–x	H 1200	Wars	
–War work–Churches	x–x	H 1200	Wars	
–War work–Elks	x–x	H 1200	Wars	
–War work–Girl Scouts	x–x	H 1200	Wars	
–War work–Red Cross	x–x	H 1200	Wars	
–War work–Salvation Army	x–x	H 1200	Wars	
–War work–Schools	x–x	H 1200	Wars	
–War work–Young Men's Christian associations	x–x	H 1200	Wars	
–War work–Young Women's Christian associations	x–x	H 1200	Wars	
–Warfare *(May Subd Geog)*	x	H 1103	Ethnic groups	
–Warrant officers	x	H 1159	Military srvces	

SUBDIVISION	SUBFIELD CODE(S)	FREE-FLOATING LIST IN SCM:SH	CATEGORY	USAGE GUIDELINES IN SCM:SH
–Wars *(May Subd Geog)*	x	H 1103	Ethnic groups	
–Waste disposal *(May Subd Geog)*	x	H 1095	see *SCM:SH*	
		H 1151.5	Types schools	
		H 1153	Industries	
–Waste minimization *(May Subd Geog)*	x	H 1095	see *SCM:SH*	
		H 1151.5	Types schools	
		H 1153	Industries	
–Watch duty	x	H 1159	Military srvces	
–Water requirements *(May Subd Geog)*	x	H 1147	Animals	
		H 1180	Plants & crops	
–Water rights	x	H 1145.5	Bodies water	
–Water-supply	x	H 1095	see *SCM:SH*	
		H 1153	Industries	
–Weapons systems	x	H 1159	Military srvces	
–Web-based instruction *(May Subd Geog)*	x	H 1095	see *SCM:SH*	
–Weed control *(May Subd Geog)*	x	H 1180	Plants & crops	
–Weight	x	H 1095	see *SCM:SH*	
		H 1147	Animals	
		H 1164	Organs of body	
–Weights and measures	x	H 1095	see *SCM:SH*	
–Weldability *(May Subd Geog)*	x	H 1158	Materials	
–Welding *(May Subd Geog)*	x	H 1149	Chemicals	
		H 1195	Land vehicles	
–Welsh authors	x	H 1156	Literatures	
–West Indian influences	x	H 1156	Literatures	H 1675
–Western influences	x	H 1156	Literatures	H 1675
–Wheels	x	H 1195	Land vehicles	
–Wheels–Alignment *(May Subd Geog)*	x–x	H 1195	Land vehicles	